The FIGHTING COLOURS *of* Richard J. Caruana

50th Anniversary Collection

4: Corpo Aereo Italiano

Battle of Britain & Russian Front

History

Concept, artwork, text and overall design:
© Richard J. Caruana

Published by:
Wydawnictwo Stratus sp.j.
Żeromskiego 4
27-600 Sandomierz
Poland

Acknowledgements:
Maurizio di Terlizzi
Giuseppe Salvagna
Pierluigi Moncalvo
Adrian M. Balch
Charles Stafrace
Godfrey Mangion
Mark Zerafa

The Regia Aeronautica's Contribution to the Battle of Britain

Italy's entry into the Second World War, declared on 10 June 1940, was a miscalculated and misguided attempt at grabbing part of the loot that would otherwise have ended up completely in the hands of the fast conquering German war machine. Following a short and ineffective cycle of operations against France it had already become apparent that Italy was ill-equipped for a modern war and lacked a clear strategy and plan of action.

Notwithstanding all this, Mussolini felt that Italy had to participate in the aerial offensive that the *Luftwaffe* was waging against Britain even though such a token force on the part of the *Regia Aeronautica* could hardly achieve any considerable impact. Moreover, the transfer of Italian units to operate across the English Channel could only have served to deplete forces far more necessary in the Mediterranean theatre. Tempting opportunities of political gains, however, won over good sense possibly believing German propaganda that was claiming that Britain was on the brink of defeat and would soon capitulate.

The *Corpo Aereo Italiano* (CAI – Italian Aviation Corps) was formed in northern Italy on 10 September 1940 consisting of two bomber *Stormi* equipped with FIAT BR.20Ms, one fighter *Stormo* equipped with FIAT CR.42s and FIAT G.50s and a reconnaissance *Squadriglia* (*Ricognizione Strategica Terrestre*) operating a small number of Cant Z.1007bis. The fighter element, in particular, was to suffer mostly; both CR.42 and G.50 were obsolete or close to obsolescence and their open cockpits were to be cause for great suffering in the colder northern European climes as pilots suffered frostbite to their hands and faces.

Once the expeditionary force had been assembled all the units began a short and limited training period hampered mostly by

FIAT CR.42 Falco M.M.5701 photograhed in September 1966 at Biggin Hill. It retains most of the colours of when it was captured, although patched up to cover the original unit codes. The yellow undersides and serial were applied during its test period. Note the front faces of the propellers in light blue grey. Also of note is the original unit badge with a blue background unlike the way it is presented today at the RAF's Battle of Britain Museum, Hendon Photo: Adrian M. Balch Collection

scarcity of fuel in northern Italy as a result of the brief campaign against France. With the training period completed, the CAI units began their ferry flights to Belgium, from where they were to operate. These flights also served to highlight the difficulties that would continually characterise the deployment of badly suited aircraft in an environment alien to that for which they had been designed to operate.

FIAT BR.20M,s from the 1ª Squadriglia (11° Gruppo, 13° Stormo}, during a mission against Britain during November 1940. M.M.21892 coded 1-6 in the foreground clearly displays the Donald Duck cartoons carried on the fuselage and on the fins. It is illustrated in profile on page 24

The FIAT BR.20M

On 10 June 1940, 172 BR.20s were on strength with the *Regia Aeronautica*, principally within the 7° *Stormo* (4° and 25° *Gruppi* based at Lonate Pozzolo), 13° *Stormo* (11° and 43° *Gruppi* at Piacenza), 18° *Stormo* (31° *Gruppo* at Aviano) and 43° *Stormo* (98° and 99° *Gruppi* at Cameri). The 43°, 7° and 13°, based in the north of Italy, participated in the short campaign against France throughout the remaining days of that month. On 13 June, 19 BR.20s from the 13° *Stormo* attacked Fayence and Hyéres.

By that time, a third of the BR.20s in service were of the new 'M' sub-type ('M' standing for 'modificato', or modified). This version was some 70cm longer than its predecessor and featured a redesigned nose with increased glazed area under the chin and a new nose turret. These modifications raised both empty and loaded weight of the aircraft resulting in a marked drop in the aircraft's performance. After testing at Lonate Pozzolo, the Borletti-Golnaghi bomb-aiming device replaced the Jozza sight.

A force of 80 BR.20Ms from 13° and 43° *Stormi* was transferred in October 1940, with the former unit taking up residence at Melsbroek while the latter was based at Chèvres. Codenames were assigned to these two airfields, the former becoming 'Dedalo' and the latter 'Icaro'. The 13° *Stormo* was under the command of *commandante* Carlo de Capoa and consisted of the 43° *Gruppo* (1ª, 3ª, 4ª, 5ª Squadriglie); the 43° *Stormo* under the command of *colonello* Luigi Questa consisted of the 98° *Gruppo* (240ª, 241ª *Squadriglie*) and 99° Gruppo (242ª, 243ª *Squadriglie*). Not all bombers arrived safely at their destination, as at least five were lost in transit after emergency landings due to bad weather. Once in Belgium the 13° and 43° *Stormi* became known as *Kampfgeschwader* 13 and 43 respectively and were incorporated within *Fliegerkorps* II.

By the 22nd of the month the force had settled down and launched its operations on the night of 24 October with an attack against Felixstowe and Harwich. *Capitano* Bassi of the 43° *Gruppo* led a formation of six BR.20Ms from his group and 12 BR.20Ms from the 13° *Stormo*. BR.20M MM21928 coded 5-8 of the 5ª *Squadriglia* crashed just after take-off near Houtem killing *capitano* Carlo Pagani and all his crew. Ten aircraft managed to locate and bomb Harwich. On the return flight MM21895 flown by *capitano* Bassi and MM22624 flown by *tenente* Pesso lost their way. All crew members safely baled out, Bassi and his crew near Cambrai and Pesso's crew between Namur and Charleroi. A third BR.20M was lost as *capitano* Machieraldo had to force land his bomber at Lillie-Epinoy.

Another mission planned for 27 October had to be cancelled and postponed to two days later with the participation of 15 BR.20Ms from the 43° *Stormo* escorted by 39 CR.42s and 34 G.50s together with a *gruppe* of Messerschmitt Bf 109Es. Engine problems forced three bombers to abort, while the rest of the raid was performed successfully during the day at the cost of one BR.20M. Five bombers were damaged by anti-aircraft fire, one of which was so badly damaged that its pilot, *maggiore* Corrado Ferretti, commander of the 241ª *Squadriglia*, had to force land the aircraft close to Kuurne; only crewman lost was 1° *aviere* Giuseppe Monti, who out of panic baled out at too low an altitude close to Courtai.

Ipswich and Harwich were attacked on the night of 5/6 November by a force of eight BR.20Ms from the 13° *Stormo* ended with one of the bombers limping home with battle damage. Ramsgate was to be the target of five Italian bombers from the 43° *Stormo* on 9 November, a raid that had to be cancelled due to bad weather. An operation planned the following day against Ipswich was also cancelled as conditions did not improve.

Harwich, where most of Britain's supplies arrived by sea, was targeted once more on the 11th. OPERAZIONE CINZANO was a well planned action in cooperation with *Luftwaffe* Ju 87s against a heavily escorted convoy in the Thames Estuary. Ten BR.20Ms led by *tenente colonnello* G. Battista Ciccu from the 99° *Gruppo* (242ª and 243ª *Squadriglie*) escorted by most of the CAI fighter element together with Bf 109Es. The G.50s and Bf 109Es encountered bad weather and were forced to abort and return to base. The Italian force approached the coast on

A crew member prepares a photographic camera before boarding for another reconnaissance sortie on the Cant Z.1007. The 172ª Squadriglia Ricognizione Stretgica operated five Cant. Z.1007s for such operations against Britain

their way to Harwich and were picked on British radar. Nos 17 and 257 Squadron Hurricanes were scrambled to intercept them while other Hurricanes from Nos 46 and 249 Squadrons airborne on patrol duties were also vectored towards them.

Heavy fighting ensued as the two forces clashed over the coast off Suffolk with the result that three bombers were shot down. BR.20M MM22267 (242-3) flown by *sottotenente* E. Squazzini and MM22620 (243-10) flown by *sottotenente* E. Bianchi were forced to ditch in the North Sea while a third, MM22621 (243-2) flown by *sottotenente* P. Appiani crashed at Tangham Forest (Woodbridge) after receiving hits from three chasing Hurricanes of No 46 Squadron. No survivors of the first two bombers were found after a search at sea by the Aldeburgh lifeboat, and by a Heinkel He 59 which was itself shown down in the process.

Survivors of Appiani's crew – himself, Degasperi, Pensa and Cerrosi – were taken prisoners while his BR.20M was taken for inspection at the Royal Aircraft Establishment, Farnborough. Three other BR.20Ms returned to base badly damaged while one Hurricane was claimed by an Italian bomber gunner during this engagement.

These raids exposed the weaknesses of the CAI showing how poorly equipped it was for the task, while fighter cover proved to be completely inadequate. During the following weeks, Great Yarmouth and Lowestoft were added to the list of targets visited and bombed but at a considerable price. During the late afternoon of 2 December 1940 a lone BR.20M from the 98° *Gruppo* flown by *capitano* Ugo Maccieraldo deviated from its course and found itself over London, where the pilot dropped his bomb load, making this the only Italian raid against the Capital City.

Enemy activity against Britain began to run down during December; the last recorded BR.20M mission was performed on 2 January 1941 with four aircraft from the 13° *Stormo* against Ipswich. Two of them dropped out due to technical problems. By the time the CAI returned home later that month, 20 BR.20Ms had been lost.

The Cant Z.1007

The 172ª *Squadriglia Ricognizione Strategica Terrestre* (strategic ground reconnaissance squadron) that was formed in September 1940 specifically to participate in operations against the British Isles consisted of five Cant Z.1007bis. These machines, under the command of *capitano* Carlo Cippo Pirelli arrived at Chievres, in Belgium, on 19 October to join the CAI where they were redesignated 172/*Aufklarungsgruppe* within *Fliegerkorps* II. The only time they went into action was during that ill-fated raid of 11 November 1940. Otherwise these bombers were relegated to liaison and transport duties in support of the fighter units.

The Fighter Element

This was composed of 50 FIAT CR.42s together with a smaller number of FIAT G.50s, both of which could be considered as obsolete or obsolescent types for that theatre of operations. The Italian biplanes were drawn from the 18° *Gruppo* (83ª, 85ª, 95ª *Squadriglie*) under the command of *maggiore* Ferruccio Vosilla that now formed part of the 56° *Stormo*.

Their transfer flights began on 19 October to the Belgian airfield at Ursel, where the crews immediately found great difficulty in adapting to the cold weather. There the fighter units became known as the *Jagdgeschwader* 56. Further training flights confirmed the poor equipment with which the Italian pilots were being obliged to face the RAF especially in the open cockpits of both CR.42 and G.50. No fighter escort was provided to the BR.20Ms during the night bombing raid against Harwich on 24 October, and the CR.42s went into action five days later escorting Italian bombers during a daylight raid against Ramsgate.

On 11 November, the 40 CR.42s escorting the bombers to Harwich were jumped upon by Hurricanes and Spitfires that shot down three Italian fighters while a further 17 were forced down just after crossing the Channel on their return, either through combat damage or due to shortage of fuel. Two more CR.42s were lost during a sortie by 29 fighters in the area between Margate and Folkstone. *Sergente* Enzo Panicchi lost his life in MM6978 of the 83a Squadriglia while sergente Antonio Lazzari flying MM6976 (85-16) was taken prisoner after he crashed his biplane near Corton Railway Station

The third CR.42, MM6876 (95-23), lost that day was flown by *sergente* Pietro Salvadori of the 95ª *Squadriglia* who performed a forced landing due to a broken oil duct on Orfordness Beach, Suffolk. The pilot was taken prisoner while the aircraft, captured with minimum damage, was later tested at Farnborough as BT474 and is now preserved (albeit in erroneous camouflage and markings) at the RAF Museum, Hendon.

According to *maggiore* Vossilla's diary, the most memorable encounter by the CAI's CR.42s was on 23 November when as soon as the Italian biplanes had crossed the British shores 14 Spitfires attacked the Italian formation. Once the initial shock of surprise had been overcome the Italian fighter pilots put up a strong resistance; Vossilla records the shooting down of five Spitfires but does not mention any losses on his side. As raids by the CAI against the British Isles came to an end on 2 January 1941 the CR.42s returned to Italy eight days later.

Although the FIAT G.50 was superior in many ways to the CR.42 biplane, it was one of the first monoplanes fighters to enter service with the *Regia Aeronautica* and had even been tested operationally during the Spanish Civil War. Adding some semblance of modernity to the CAI, the 48 G.50s were formed into the 20º *Gruppo* (351ª, 352ª, 353ª *Squadriglie*) of the 56º *Stormo* under the command of *maggiore* Mario Bonzano as part of the fighter element.

After a lengthy transfer and training period, operations started on 24 October escorting bombers on a raid against the port of Harwich. The FIAT monoplanes were in action also on 29 October, when 34 G.50s provided escort to the bombers raiding Ramsgate.

Neither G.50 nor CR.42 were equipped with any cockpit heating, or facilities for heated pilot suits. This caused considerable discomfort, as pilots flew in freezing sub-zero temperatures, resulting in severe cases of frostbite to hands and faces. Only three of the G.50s were equipped with radio and none had instrumental navigation equipment. All pilots exchanged their inadequate cork-filled life-vests with inflatable rubber vests supplied by their German allies.

On 1 November 1940 26 G.50s flew a fighter sweep over Canterbury where they were met with heavy anti-aircraft fire. Luckily they did not encounter RAF fighters and all

FIAT CR.42, M.M.5701, flown by sergente pilota Pietro Salvadori, 95ª Squadriglia, 18º Gruppo, 56º Stormo standing on its nose. The pilot was forced to force land the aircraft on 11 November 1940 due to a burst oil pipe on Ordfordness Beach (Suffolk), and was taken prisoner. The aircraft now resides in the RAF Museum, Hendon

The scene at Maldegem (Belgium), in November 1940 with FIAT CR.42s neatly parked on their hard standing being prepared for a sortie. Inclement weather of that 1940-41 winter severly limited the operations of these aircraft, especially due to the open cockpits and lack of heated flying suits for the pilots

FIAT G.50s being services at Ursel (Belgium) in October 1940. In the background is M.M.5372 belonging to the Commander of the 20º Gruppo, maggiore Mario Bonzano. The rough finish of these aircraft is attributed to lack of application of a primer suited for cold weather operations, and possibly also due to contraction of the metal airframe

returned to base. A week later 22 G.50s did come across four RAF fighters as they flew an offensive patrol between Dungness, Folkstone, Canterbury and Margate. A claim was made that day by the Italians of having shot down Spitfire P7377 of No 19 Squadron which had to perform an emergency landing but in fact no combat has ever been recorded between the G.50s and British fighters.

In support of the main attack of 11 November, five Cant Z.1007s of the 172ª *Squadriglia* performed a diversion to Great Yarmouth escorted by 24 G.50s of the 20º *Gruppo*, without meeting any opposition. On the 23rd of that month No 92 Squadron Spitfires reported spotting Bf 109Es around midday south of Dover but these were more likely G.50s who, however, avoided engagement. G.50s were out again for an offensive patrol over Ashford, Maidstone and Dungness on 28 November together with 15 CR.42s and some Bf 109Es, again without meeting opposition.

Around the third week of December 1940 the *Stato Maggiore* of the *Regia Aeronautica* ordered the return of the CAI to Italy. Although officially it was termed as a temporary measure due to deteriorating weather conditions it was in fact forced to take such a step due to pressure that Italian forces were suffering on other fronts, particularly in the operations against Greece and the British advance in North Africa.

Although elements of the CAI began their return journey to Italy on 10 January 1941 two *squadriglie* of G.50s (352ª, 353ª) were left behind to perform patrol duties over the Belgian, French and Dutch coasts. For this purpose the two units moved to Desvres in France on 1 March 1941. Some of the Italian pilots became familiar with the Bf 109E, flying at JG51's training unit based at Cazaux (France). One of them was *capitano* Furio Niclot Doglio, later to become an important fighter ace of the *Regia Aeronautica*. Needless to say, the G.50 pilots were tremendously impressed by the Messerschmitt fighter's qualities. A request for the German fighter to be supplied to Italy was turned down, however.

Unfortunately the 20º *Gruppo* suffered a couple of losses during this period, the first being on 3 April 1941 when *sergente maggiore pilota* Remo Meneghini of the 252ª *Squadriglia* lost his life in a flying accident whilst on patrol. On 13 April *tenente* Mario Roncalli of the 352ª *Squadriglia* lost control and crashed to his death after having been alerted to intercept, without success, an enemy aircraft over East Flanders. This was a few days before the 20º *Gruppo* was ordered to fly back to Italy on 16 April 1941, and then on to Libya.

Colour Art - Battle of Britain

FIAT CR.42 Falco, *M.M.4462/95, flown by maggiore Francesco Vossilla, Commander of the 18º Gruppo, 56º Stormo, as it appeared a few days before leaving for Belgium. Giallo Mimetico (FS.30266), Verde Mimetico (FS.34102) and Marrone Mimetico (FS.30219) upper surfaces with Aluminio (FS.17178) undersides. Inter-plane struts in Grigio Azzurro Chiaro (FS.26307). Codes in light blue-grey with black drop shadow over a wide white fuselage band. Serial in white (FIAT CR.42 in white with blue FS.25095 shadow). National fasces markings in black, over a white background, above top and below lower wings. Rank pennant below cockpit*

FIAT CR.42 Falco, *M.M.4332/95-1, flown by capitano Gino Lodi, Commander of the 95ª Squadriglia, 18º Gruppo, 56º Stormo, transiting through Frankfurt to Belgium, October 1940. Giallo Mimetico, Verde Mimetico and Marrone Mimetico upper surfaces with Aluminio undersides. Inter-plane struts in Grigio Azzurro Chiaro. Codes in light blue-grey with black drop shadow. Serial in white (FIAT CR.42 in white with blue FS.25095 shadow). National fasces markings in black, over a white background, above top and below lower wings. Rank pennant below cockpit, white spinner*

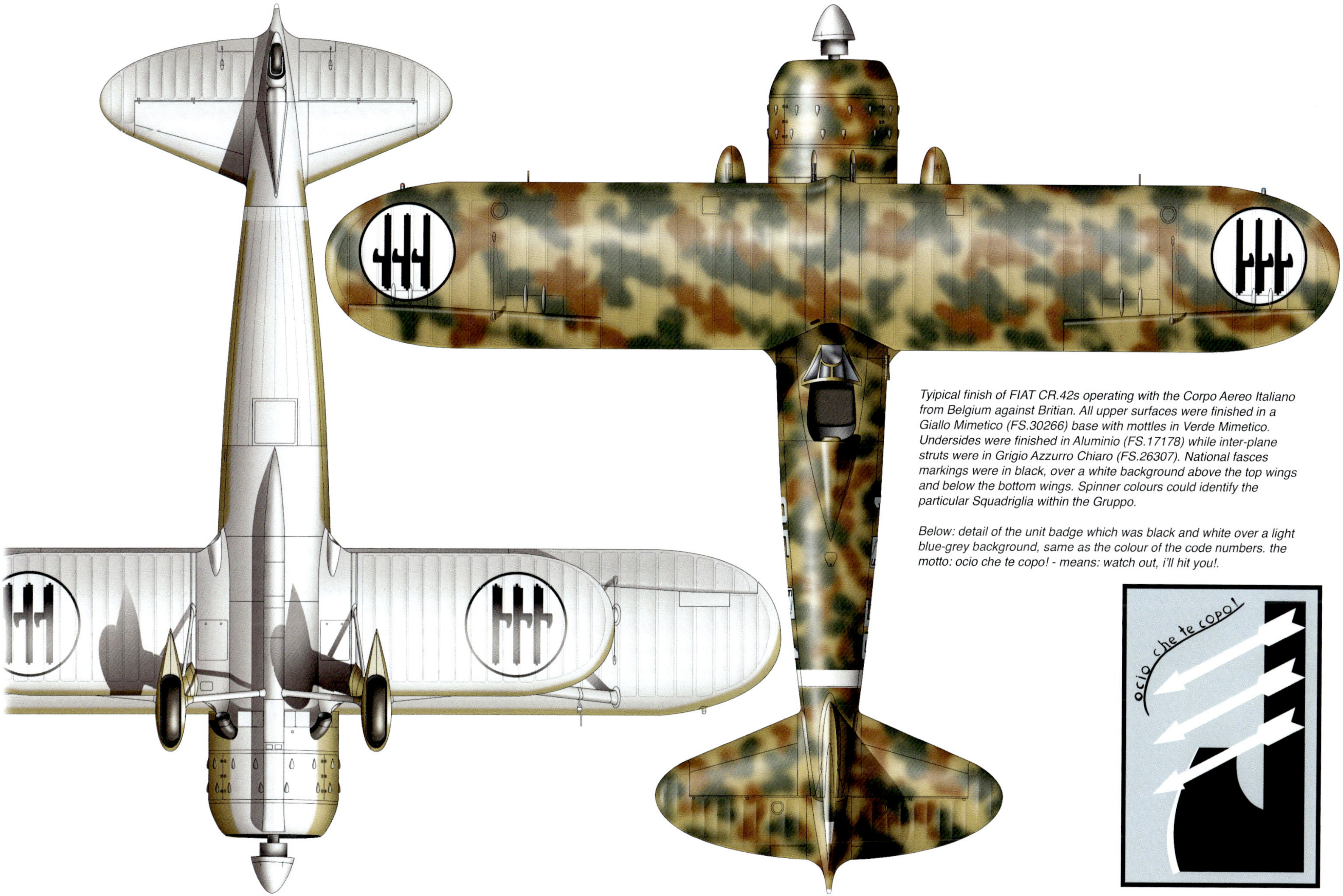

Typical finish of FIAT CR.42s operating with the Corpo Aereo Italiano from Belgium against Britian. All upper surfaces were finished in a Giallo Mimetico (FS.30266) base with mottles in Verde Mimetico. Undersides were finished in Aluminio (FS.17178) while inter-plane struts were in Grigio Azzurro Chiaro (FS.26307). National fasces markings were in black, over a white background above the top wings and below the bottom wings. Spinner colours could identify the particular Squadriglia within the Gruppo.

Below: detail of the unit badge which was black and white over a light blue-grey background, same as the colour of the code numbers. the motto: ocio che te copo! - means: watch out, i'll hit you!.

FIAT CR.42 Falco, *M.M.5667/83-1, flown by capitano Molinari, Commander 83ª Squadriglia, 18º Gruppo, 56º Stormo, CAI, Ursel (Belgium), November 1940. Giallo Mimetico, Verde Mimetico and Marrone Mimetico upper surfaces with Aluminio undersides. Interplane struts in Grigio Azzurro Chiaro . Codes in light blue-grey with black drop shadow. Serial in white (FIAT CR.42 in white with blue shadow). Yellow spinner and front of engine cowling. National fasces markings in black, over a white background, above top and below lower wings*

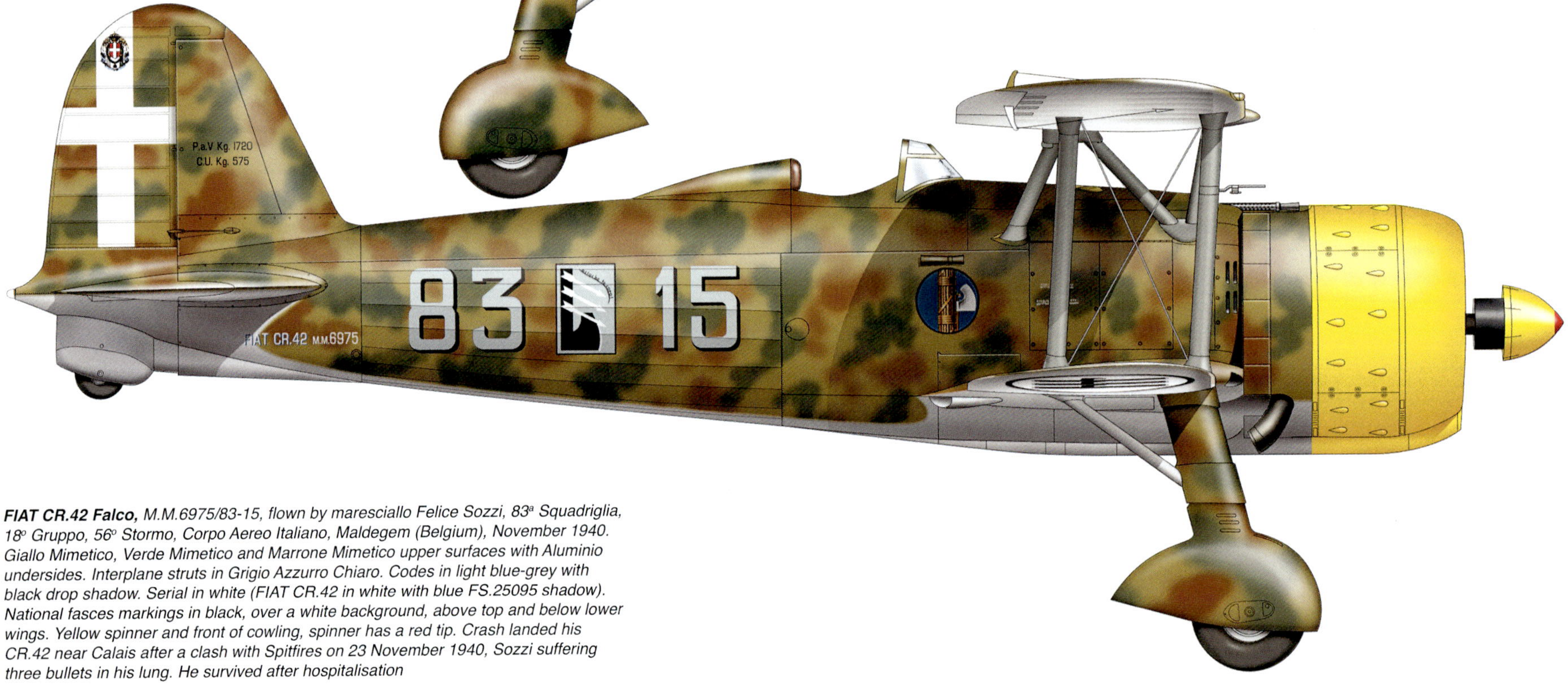

FIAT CR.42 Falco, *M.M.6975/83-15, flown by maresciallo Felice Sozzi, 83ª Squadriglia, 18º Gruppo, 56º Stormo, Corpo Aereo Italiano, Maldegem (Belgium), November 1940. Giallo Mimetico, Verde Mimetico and Marrone Mimetico upper surfaces with Aluminio undersides. Interplane struts in Grigio Azzurro Chiaro. Codes in light blue-grey with black drop shadow. Serial in white (FIAT CR.42 in white with blue FS.25095 shadow). National fasces markings in black, over a white background, above top and below lower wings. Yellow spinner and front of cowling, spinner has a red tip. Crash landed his CR.42 near Calais after a clash with Spitfires on 23 November 1940, Sozzi suffering three bullets in his lung. He survived after hospitalisation*

FIAT CR.42 Falco, *M.M.5668/83-2, 83ª Squadriglia, 18° Gruppo, 56° Stormo, CAI, November 1940. Giallo Mimetico and Verde Mimetico upper surfaces with Aluminio undersides (Marrone Mimetico (FS.30219) possibly added to the top wing colours). Inter-plane struts in Grigio Azzurro Chiaro. Codes in light blue-grey with black drop shadow. Serial in white (FIAT CR.42 in white with blue FS.25095 shadow). National fasces markings in black, over a white background, above top and below lower wings. Red spinner, yellow front of cowling*

FIAT CR.42 Falco, *M.M.5680/85-4, flown by tenente 'Peppo' Re, 85ª Squadriglia, 18° Gruppo, 56° Stormo, CAI, Ursel (Belgium), mid-November 1940. Giallo Mimetico and Verde Mimetico upper surfaces with Aluminio undersides (Marrone Mimetico added to the top wing colours). Inter-plane struts in Grigio Azzurro Chiaro. Codes in light blue-grey with black drop shadow. Serial in white (FIAT CR.42 in white with blue FS.25095 shadow). National fasces markings in black, over a white background, above top and below lower wings. Yellow spinner and front of cowling*

FIAT CR.42 Falco, *M.M.4326/85-9, 85ª Squadriglia, 18° Gruppo, 56° Stormo, CAI, Maldegem (Belgium), November 1940. Giallo Mimetico, Verde Mimetico and Marrone Mimetico upper surfaces with Aluminio undersides. Inter-plane struts in Grigio Azzurro Chiaro. Codes in light blue-grey with black drop shadow. Serial in white (FIAT CR.42 in white with blue FS.25095 shadow). National fasces markings in black, over a white background, above top and below lower wings. Yellow spinner, front of engine cowling and mid fuselage band*

FIAT CR.42 Falco, *M.M.6976/85-16, flown by sergente Antonio Lazzari, 85ª Squadriglia, 18° Gruppo, 56° Stormo, Corpo Aereo Italiano, Maldegem (Belgium), November 1940. Giallo Mimetico 3, Verde Mimetico 3 and Marrone Mimetico 3 uppersufaces with Grigio Mimetico undersides; yellow front of cowling and spinner, the latter with a red tip. Codes in light blue-grey, thinly outlined and shadowed in black. Serial in white (FIAT CR.42 in white with blue FS.25095 shadow). National fasces markings in black, over a white background, above top and below lower wings. Note that this CR.42 was equipped with radio. Shot down on 11 November 1940 near Corton Railway Station*

FIAT CR.42 Falco, *M.M.6969/85-17, 85ª Squadriglia, 18° Gruppo, 56° Stormo, CAI, Maldegem (Belgium), November 1940. Giallo Mimetico, Verde Mimetico and Marrone Mimetico upper surfaces with Aluminio undersides. Interplane struts in Grigio Azzurro Chiaro. Codes in light blue-grey with black drop shadow. Serial in white (FIAT CR.42 in white with blue FS.25095 shadow). National fasces markings in black, over a white background, above top and below lower wings. Yellow spinner and front of cowling*

FIAT CR.42 Falco, *M.M.5699/85-12, flown by sergente Cavallar, 85ª Squadriglia, 18° Gruppo, 56° Stormo, CAI, Belgium, November 1940. Giallo Mimetico and Verde Mimetico upper surfaces with Aluminio undersides (Marrone Mimetico possibly added to the top wing colours). Inter-plane struts in Grigio Azzurro Chiaro. Codes in light blue-grey with black drop shadow. Serial in white (FIAT CR.42 in white with blue FS.25095 shadow). National fasces markings in black, over a white background, above top and below lower wings. Green spinner. This is how 85-12 appeared on arriving in Belgium when Cavallari ground looped his CR.42 which ended on its nose*

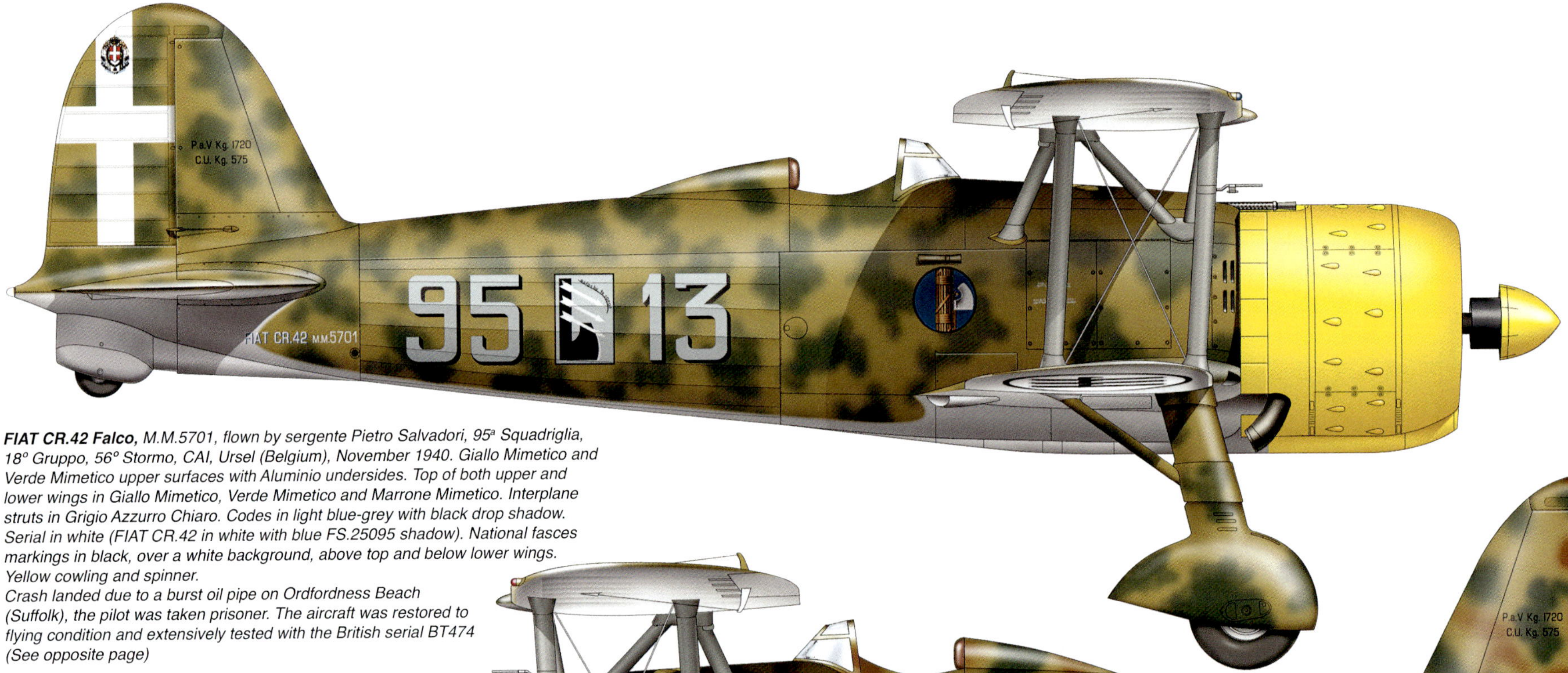

FIAT CR.42 Falco, *M.M.5701, flown by sergente Pietro Salvadori, 95ª Squadriglia, 18° Gruppo, 56° Stormo, CAI, Ursel (Belgium), November 1940. Giallo Mimetico and Verde Mimetico upper surfaces with Aluminio undersides. Top of both upper and lower wings in Giallo Mimetico, Verde Mimetico and Marrone Mimetico. Interplane struts in Grigio Azzurro Chiaro. Codes in light blue-grey with black drop shadow. Serial in white (FIAT CR.42 in white with blue FS.25095 shadow). National fasces markings in black, over a white background, above top and below lower wings. Yellow cowling and spinner.*
Crash landed due to a burst oil pipe on Ordfordness Beach (Suffolk), the pilot was taken prisoner. The aircraft was restored to flying condition and extensively tested with the British serial BT474 (See opposite page)

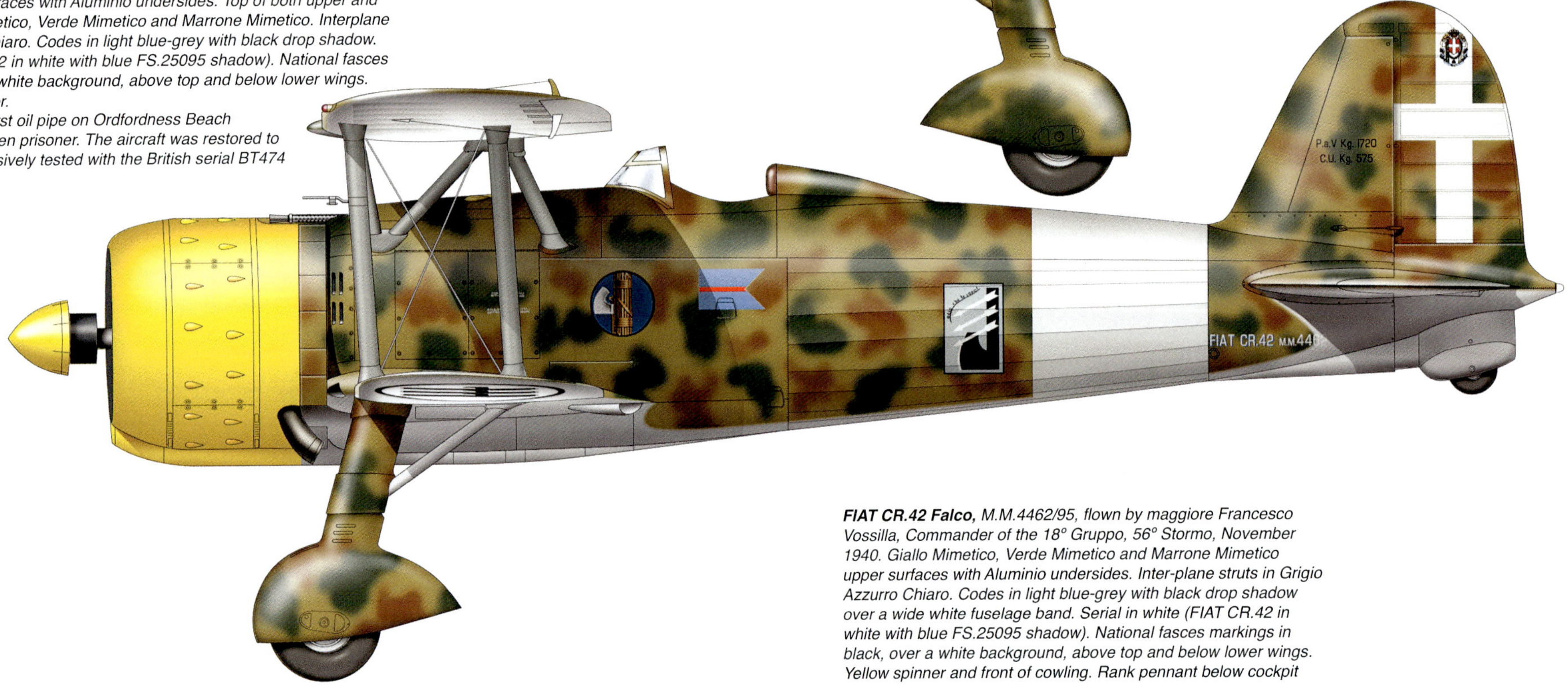

FIAT CR.42 Falco, *M.M.4462/95, flown by maggiore Francesco Vossilla, Commander of the 18° Gruppo, 56° Stormo, November 1940. Giallo Mimetico, Verde Mimetico and Marrone Mimetico upper surfaces with Aluminio undersides. Inter-plane struts in Grigio Azzurro Chiaro. Codes in light blue-grey with black drop shadow over a wide white fuselage band. Serial in white (FIAT CR.42 in white with blue FS.25095 shadow). National fasces markings in black, over a white background, above top and below lower wings. Yellow spinner and front of cowling. Rank pennant below cockpit*

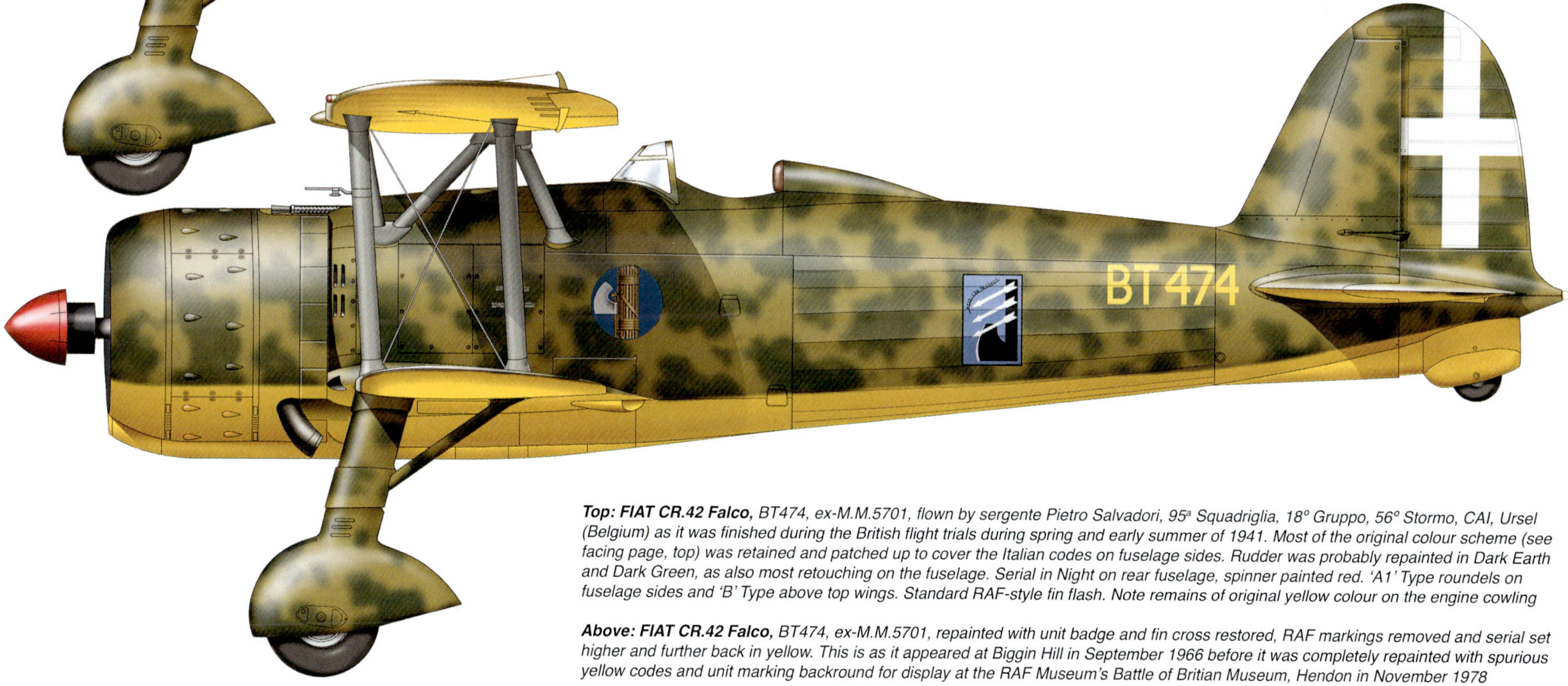

***Top:* FIAT CR.42 Falco,** *BT474, ex-M.M.5701, flown by sergente Pietro Salvadori, 95ª Squadriglia, 18º Gruppo, 56º Stormo, CAI, Ursel (Belgium) as it was finished during the British flight trials during spring and early summer of 1941. Most of the original colour scheme (see facing page, top) was retained and patched up to cover the Italian codes on fuselage sides. Rudder was probably repainted in Dark Earth and Dark Green, as also most retouching on the fuselage. Serial in Night on rear fuselage, spinner painted red. 'A1' Type roundels on fuselage sides and 'B' Type above top wings. Standard RAF-style fin flash. Note remains of original yellow colour on the engine cowling*

***Above:* FIAT CR.42 Falco,** *BT474, ex-M.M.5701, repainted with unit badge and fin cross restored, RAF markings removed and serial set higher and further back in yellow. This is as it appeared at Biggin Hill in September 1966 before it was completely repainted with spurious yellow codes and unit marking backround for display at the RAF Museum's Battle of Britian Museum, Hendon in November 1978*

FIAT G.50 Freccia, *M.M.5372/20°GR, flown by maggiore Mario Bonzano, Commander of the XX° Gruppo, 56° Stormo (known as 20./JG56 by the Luftwaffe), CAI, Ursel (Belgium) October 1940. Giallo Mimetico1, Verde Mimetico 1 and Marrone Mimetico 2 uppersurfaces; Grigio Mimetico undersides. Yellow (possibly RLM 04) cowl front and spinner; command pennant aft of cockpit. No national markings above the wings. The finish of FIAT G.50s operating in this theatre suffered extensively from weathering with paint flaked off on extensive areas of the fuselage; these profiles are shown with the aircraft in complete finish without weathering for clarity*

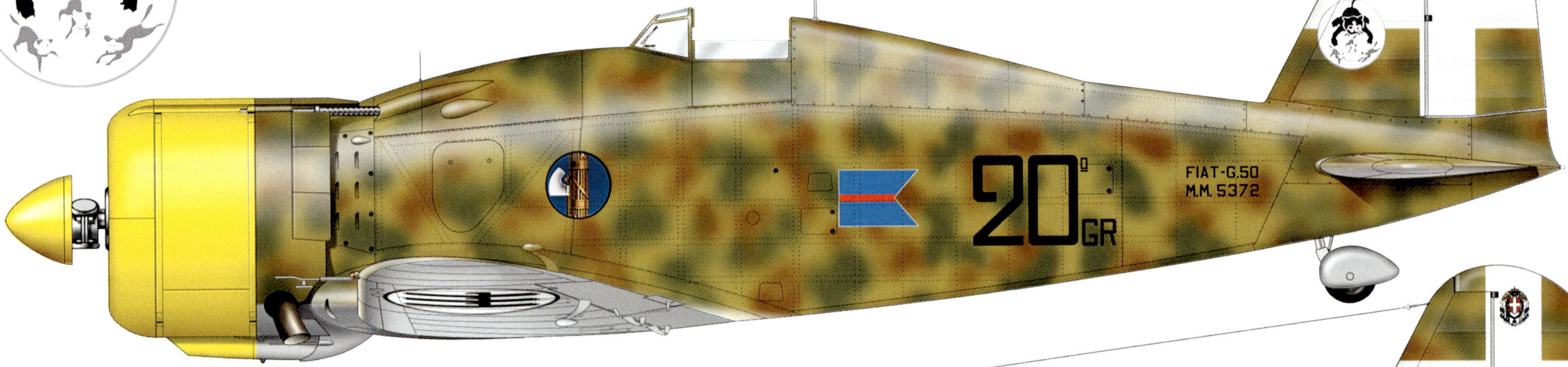

FIAT G.50 Freccia, *M.M.5372/20°GR, flown by maggiore Mario Bonzano, Commander of the XX° Gruppo, 56° Stormo with a wide fuselage band in yellow added to the centre*

***FIAT G.50 Freccia**, 351-2, 351ª Squadriglia (20° Gruppo, 56° Stormo), CAI, Ursel (Belgium), November 1940. Giallo Mimetico 3 with Verde Mimetico 3 and Marrone Mimetico 2 mottling on all upper surfaces; Grigio Mimetico undersides. White spinner, yellow fuselage band; code is in black (351) and red (2). Standard fasces wing markings without white background. below the wings only. Unit badge on fin (both sides)*

***FIAT G.50 Freccia**, 352-1, 352ª Squadriglia, 20° Gruppo, 56° Stormo, CAI, Belgium, October 1940. Giallo Mimetico 3, Verde Mimetico 3, Marrone Mimetico 2 upper surfaces with Grigio Mimetico undersides; black/red codes. White background to wing markings under the wings, no national markings above wings; unit badge on fin (both sides)*

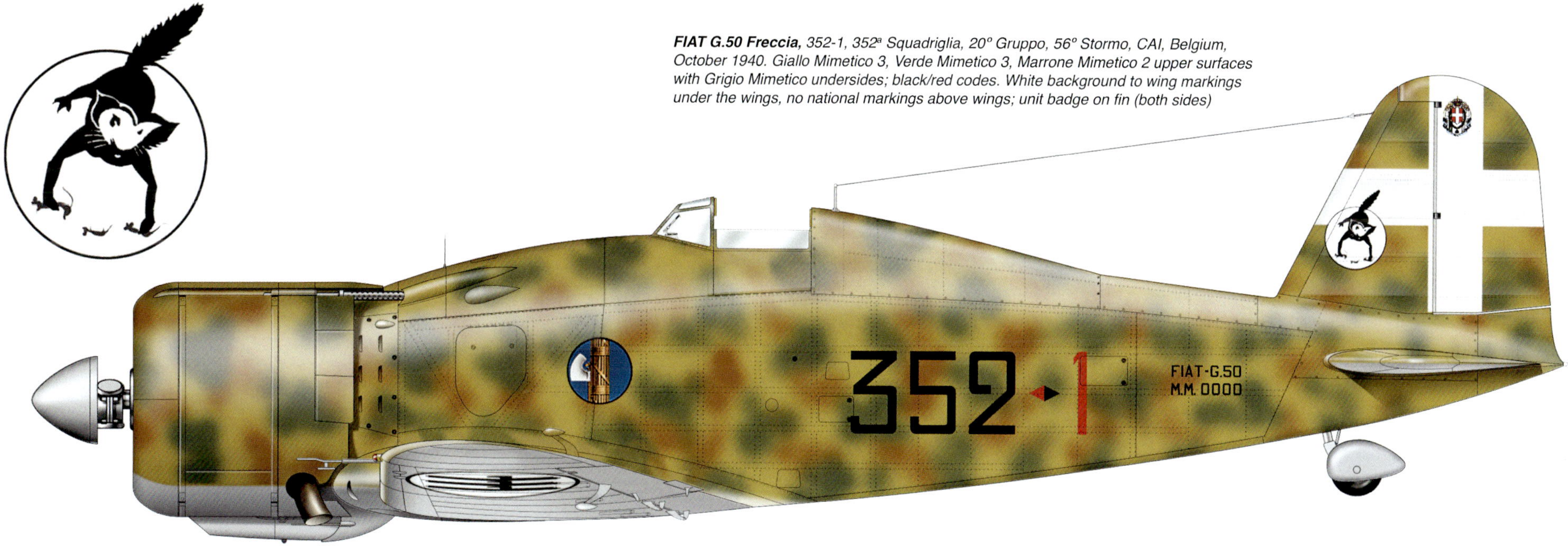

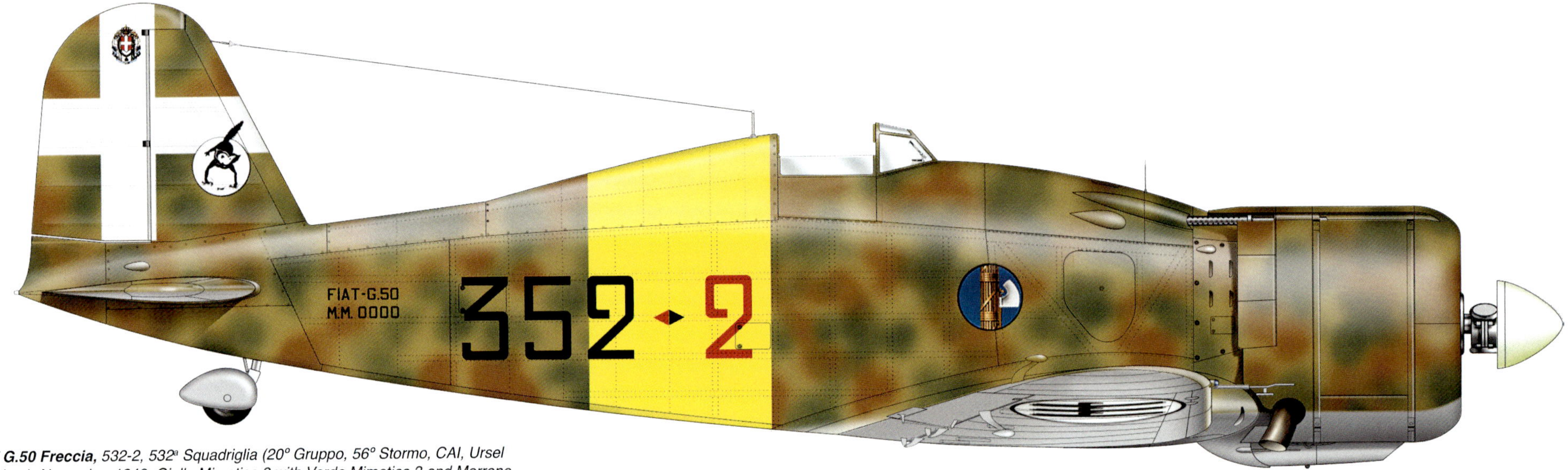

FIAT G.50 Freccia, *532-2, 532ª Squadriglia (20° Gruppo, 56° Stormo, CAI, Ursel (Belgium), November 1940. Giallo Mimetico 3 with Verde Mimetico 3 and Marrone Mimetico 2 mottling on all upper surfaces; Grigio Mimetico undersides. White spinner, yellow fuselage band; code is in black (351) and red (2). Standard fasces wing markings without white background*

FIAT G.50 Freccia, *532-5, 532ª Squadriglia (20° Gruppo, 56° Stormo, CAI, Ursel (Belgium), November 1940. Giallo Mimetico 3 with Verde Mimetico 3 and Marrone Mimetico 2 mottling on all upper surfaces; Grigio Mimetico undersides. White spinner, yellow fuselage band; code is in black (351) and red (2). Standard fasces wing markings without white background*

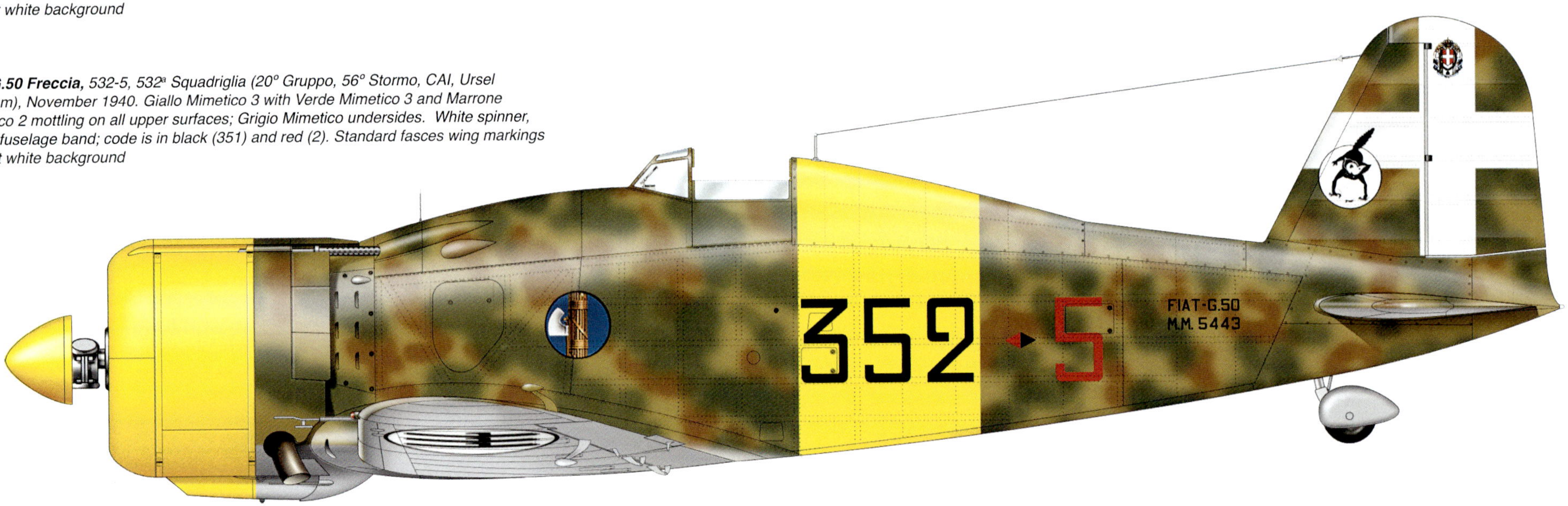

FIAT G.50 Freccia, *352-7, 352ª Squadriglia, 20° Gruppo, 56° Stormo, CAI, Ursel-Belgium, late 1940. Giallo Mimetico 3, Verde Mimetico 3, Marrone Mimetico 2 upper surfaces with Grigio Mimetico undersides, Black/red codes; yellow cowling front, white spinner. White background to wing markings under the wings, no national markings above wings; unit badge on fin (both sides). Note no cover on tailwheel*

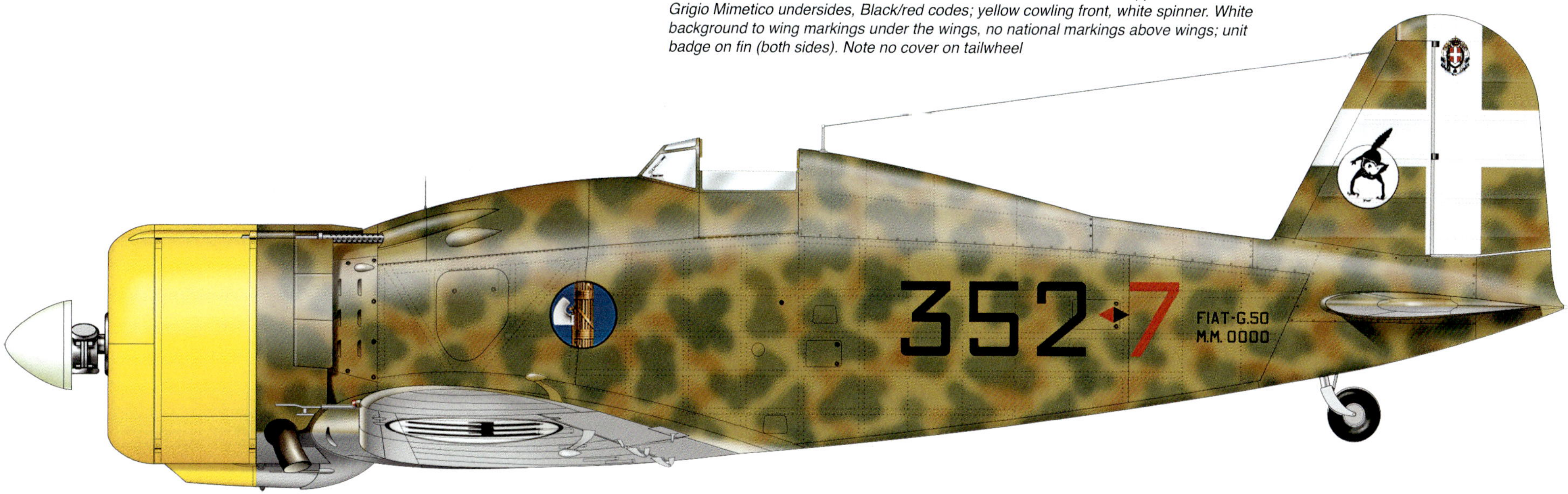

FIAT G.50 Freccia, *352-10, 352ª Squadriglia, 20° Gruppo, 56° Stormo, CAI, Belgium, October 1940. Giallo Mimetico 3, Verde Mimetico 3, Marrone Mimetico 2 upper surfaces with Grigio Mimetico undersides; black/red codes. White background to wing markings under the wings, no national markings above wings. Giallo Cromo front of cowling and spinner*

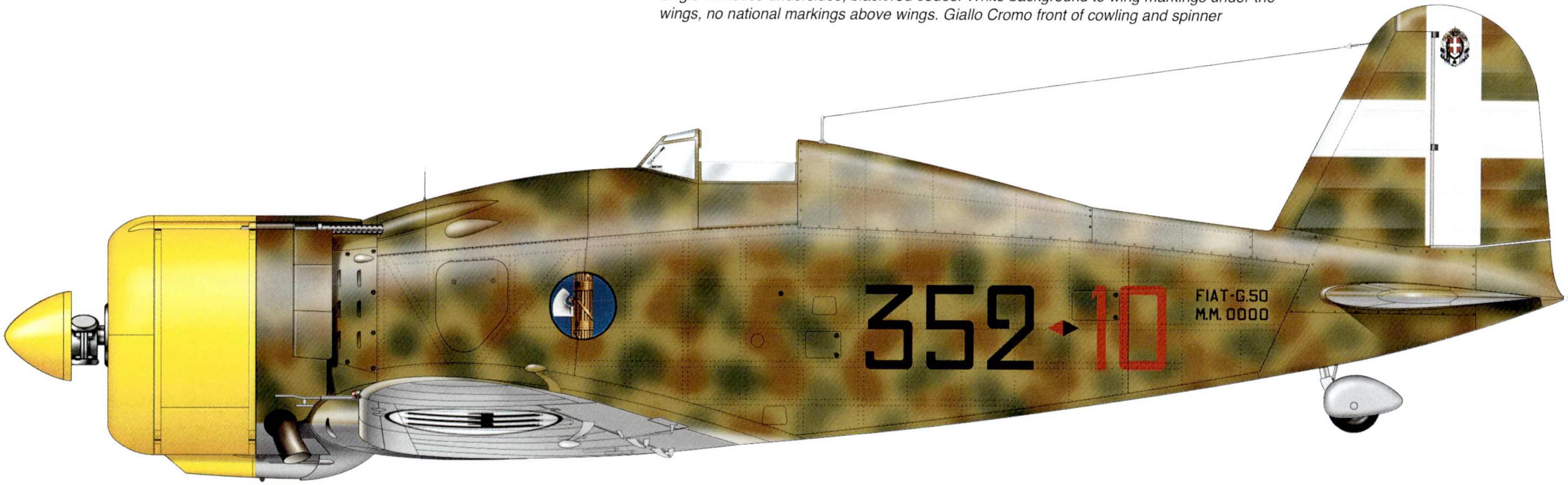

FIAT G.50 Freccia, *M.M.5403. 352-13, 352ª Squadriglia, 20° Gruppo, 56° Stormo, CAI, Belgium, October 1940. Giallo Mimetico 3, Verde Mimetico 3, Marrone Mimetico 2 upper surfaces with Grigio Mimetico undersides; black/red codes. Giallo Cromo spinner and front of cowling; white background to wing markings under the wings, no national markings above wings. Unit badge on fin (both sides)*

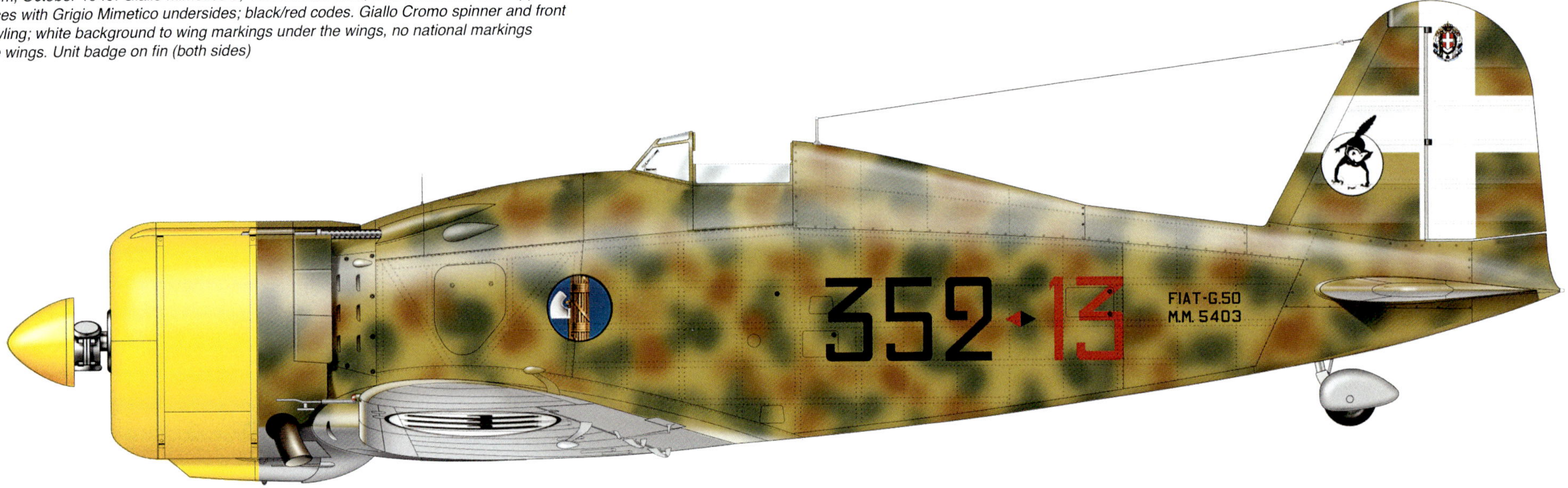

FIAT G.50 Freccia, *353-7, 35ª Squadriglia, 20° Gruppo, 56° Stormo, CAI, Belgium, October 1940. Giallo Mimetico 3, Verde Mimetico 3, Marrone Mimetico 2 upper surfaces with Grigio Mimetico undersides; black/red codes. White background to wing markings under the wings, no national markings above wings; unit badge on fin (both sides)*

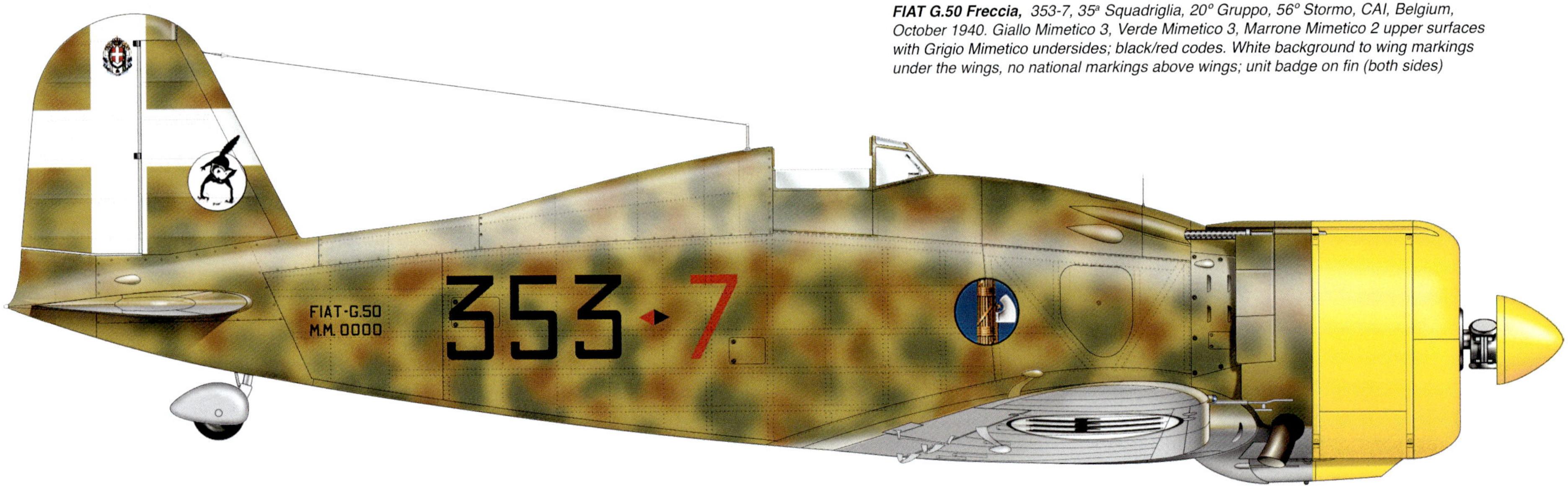

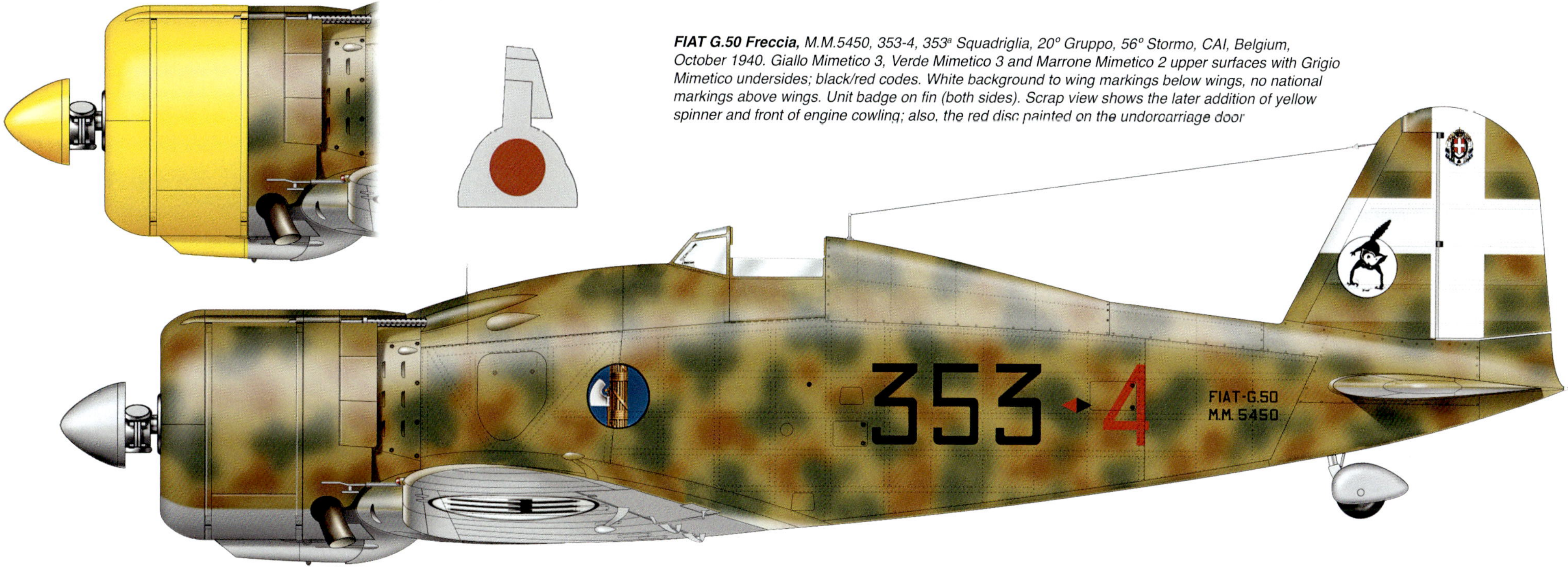

FIAT G.50 Freccia, *M.M.5450, 353-4, 353ª Squadriglia, 20º Gruppo, 56º Stormo, CAI, Belgium, October 1940. Giallo Mimetico 3, Verde Mimetico 3 and Marrone Mimetico 2 upper surfaces with Grigio Mimetico undersides; black/red codes. White background to wing markings below wings, no national markings above wings. Unit badge on fin (both sides). Scrap view shows the later addition of yellow spinner and front of engine cowling; also, the red disc painted on the undercarriage door*

FIAT G.50 Freccia, *M.M.5372, flown by maggiore Mario Bonzano, Commander of the XXº Gruppo (56º Stormo – known as 20./JG56 by the Luftwaffe), Corpo Aerea Italiano, Maldegem (Belgium), January 1941. Giallo Mimetico uppersurfaces with Verde Mimetico 1 and Marrone Mimetico mottling; Grigio Mimetico undersides. Yellow cowl front and spinner, white angled band around rear fuselage; note command pennant aft of cockpit. It appears that this aircraft had been completely repainted before its re-entry to Italy, the white band indicating that the unit was preparing for deployment in the Mediterranean. Other G.50s appearing in the same photo on which this profiles is based remain in their normal CAI finish, with yellow cowls and no fuselage bands*

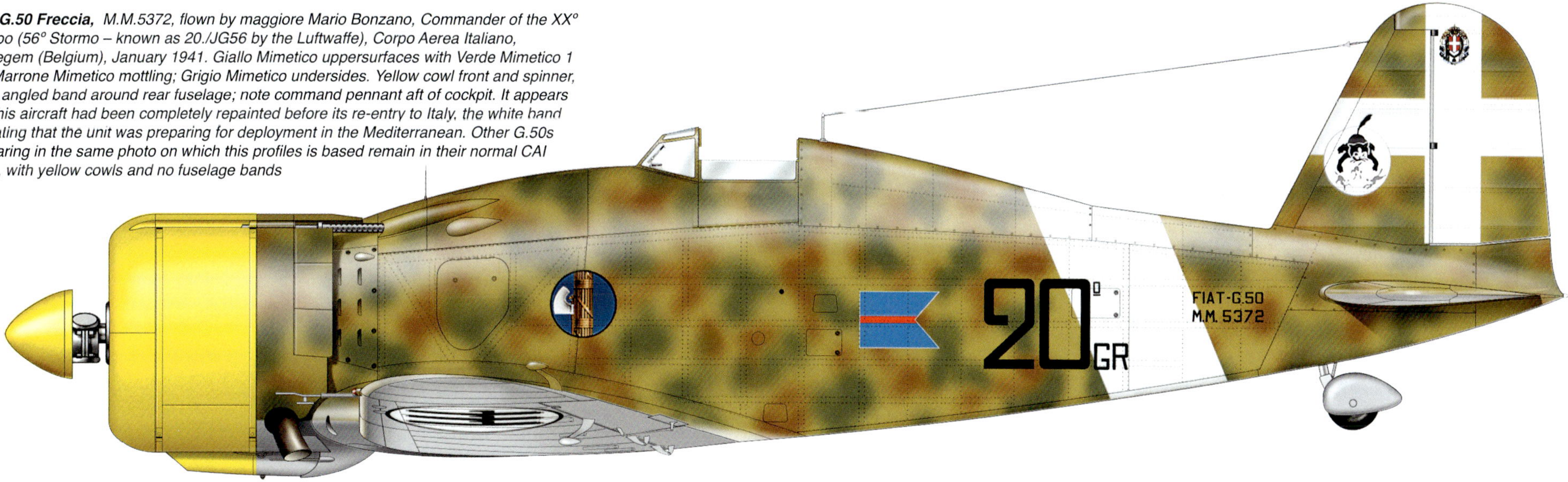

***Cant Z.1007bis Alcione**, M.M.24256/172-5, 172ª Squadriglia RST, CAI, Chièvres (Belgium), October 1940. Giallo Mimetico, Marrone Mimetico and Verde Mimetico uppersurfaces with Grigio Azzurro Chiaro undersides. Yellow fuselage band; wing markings in black only on top and white on black underneath. Code in black and red; Unit marking on fuselage sides*

***Cant Z.1007bis Alcione**, M.M.22148/172-4, 172ª Squadriglia Ricognizione Strategica Terrestre, CAI, Chièvres (Belgium), October 1940. Giallo Mimetico 3, Marrone Mimetico 2 and Verde Mimetico 3 uppersurfaces with Grigio Mimetico undersides. Wing markings with white background above and white on black underneath. Code in black and red; unit marking on fuselage sides (both sides)*

***Cant Z.1007bis Alcione**, M.M.22144/172-2, 172ª Squadriglia Ricognizione Strategica Terrestre, CAI, January 1841. Giallo Mimetico 3, Marrone Mimetico 2 and Verde Mimetico 3 uppersurfaces with Grigio Mimetico undersides. Wing markings with white background above and white on black underneath. Code in black and red; unit marking on fuselage sides (both sides). Crashed at Frankfurt (Germany) on 11 January 1941 as the CAI was returning back to Italy at the end of operations against Britain*

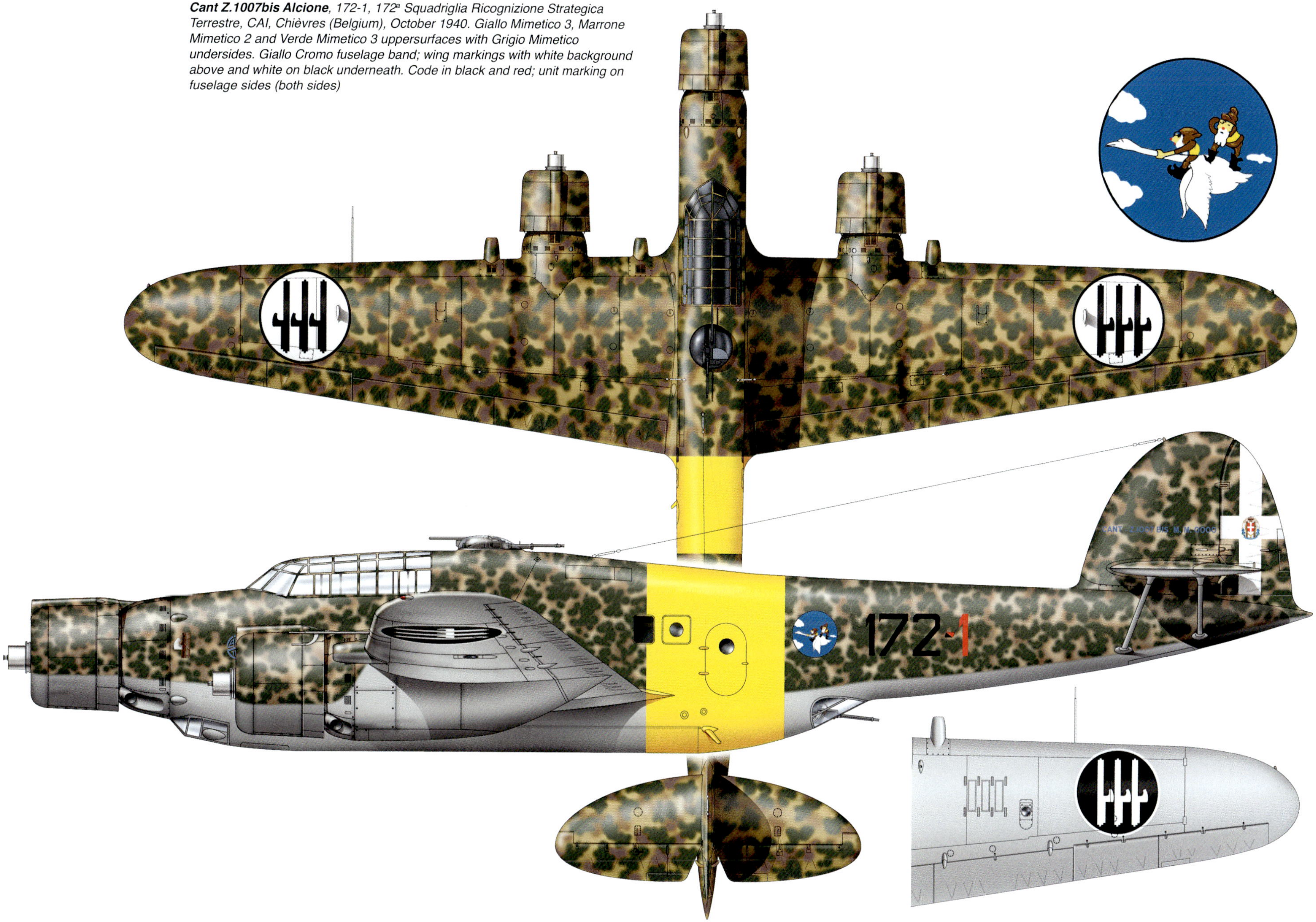

Cant Z.1007bis Alcione, *172-1, 172ª Squadriglia Ricognizione Strategica Terrestre, CAI, Chièvres (Belgium), October 1940. Giallo Mimetico 3, Marrone Mimetico 2 and Verde Mimetico 3 uppersurfaces with Grigio Mimetico undersides. Giallo Cromo fuselage band; wing markings with white background above and white on black underneath. Code in black and red; unit marking on fuselage sides (both sides)*

FIAT BR.20M Cicogna, *M.M.21892/1-6, 1ª Squadriglia, 11° Gruppo, 13° Stormo, Melsbroek (Belgium), November 1940. Giallo Mimetico 3, Verde Mimetico 3 and Marrone Mimetico 2 upper surfaces; Grigio Mimetico undersides. White background to national markings in four wing positions. '6' repeated on nose; note two version of 'Donald Duck', one on fuselage and another on fin*

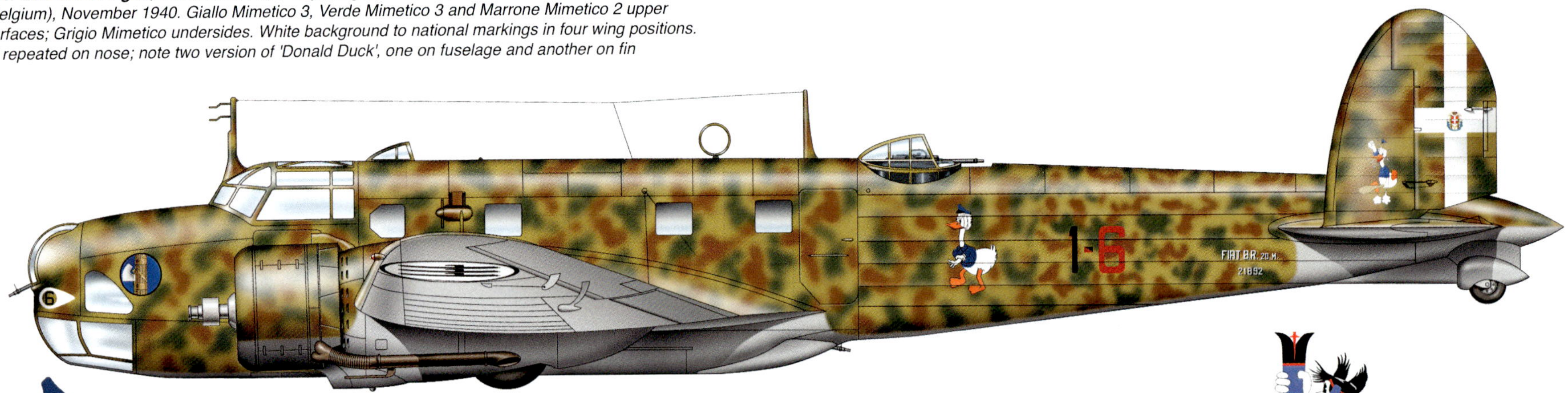

FIAT BR.20M Cicogna, *M.M.21893/3-1, 3ª Squqadriglia, 43° Gruppo, 13° Stormo BT, CAI, Melsbroek (Belgium), October 1940. Giallo Mimetico 3, Verde Mimetico 3 and Marrone Mimetico 2 upper surfaces with Grigio Mimetico undersides. Codes in black and red, serial in white with black drop shadow. 'La Torbida' badge carried aft of the fuselage access door. Black 'teardrop' on nose with red '1'. Note that the House of Savoy emblem is carried at the centre of the cross rather than high up, as usual*

FIAT BR.20M Cicogna, *M.M.22259/3-7, 3ª Squadriglia, 43° Gruppo, 13° Stormo BT, CAI, Melsbroek (Belgium), October 1940. Giallo Mimetico 3, Verde Mimetico 3 and Marrone Mimetico 2 upper surfaces with Grigio Mimetico undersides. Note code colours have been switched and the House of Savoy emblem is carried high on the cross. "La Torbida' carried aft of crew access door. Red '7' within a black teardrop on nose*

FIAT BR.20M Cicogna, *M.M.22264/3-9, 3ª Squqadriglia, 43° Gruppo, 13° Stormo BT, CAI, Melsbroek (Belgium), October 1940. Giallo Mimetico 3, Verde Mimetico 3 and Marrone Mimetico 2 upper surfaces with Grigio Mimetico undersides. Black/red codes, serial in white with black drop shadow. 'La Torbida' badge carried aft of the fuselage access door with a Yellow fuselage band. Black 'teardrop' with red '9' on nose*

Detail of the bumble bee on the 'Pluto' unit badge had its yellow/black striped body turned into a Union Jack during the operations against Britain

FIAT BR.20M Cicogna, *M.M.21894/4-7, 4ª Squadriglia. 11° Gruppo., 13° Stormo, Corpo Aereo Italiano, Melsbroek, Belgium. Giallo Mimetico 3 upper surface with mottling in Verde Mimetico 3 and Marrone Mimetico; Grigio Azzurro Chiaro undersides. National markings with white backing in four wing positions*

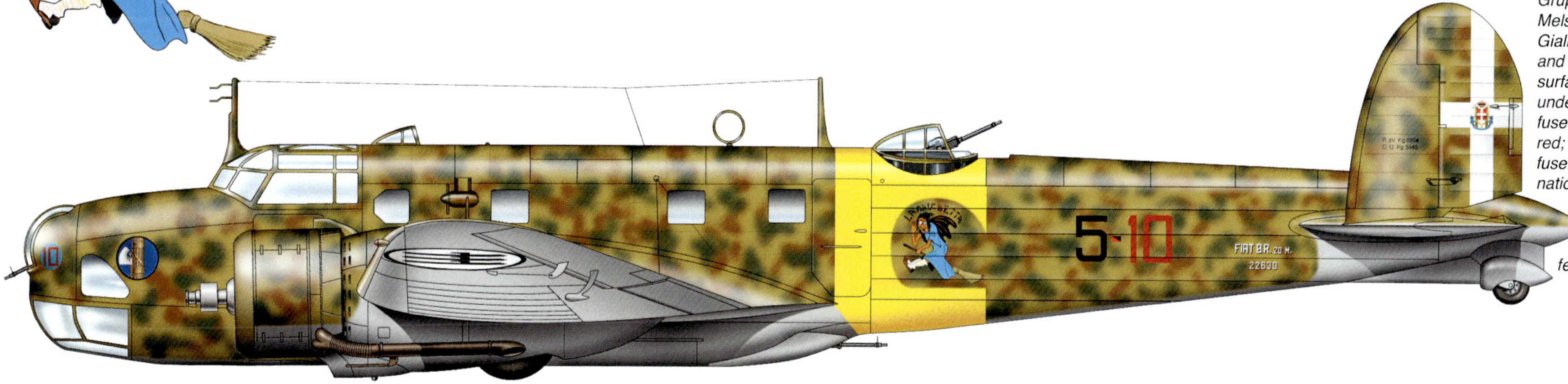

Left: FIAT BR.20M Cicogna, *M.M.22630/5-10, flown by tenente Dino Bossi, 5ª Squadriglia, 43° Gruppo, 13° Stormo BT, CAI, Melsbroek (Belgium), October 1940. Giallo Mimetico 3, Verde Mimetico 3 and Marrone Mimetic 2 upper surfaces with Grigio Mimetico undersides; Giallo Cromo mid-fuselage band. Codes in black and red; 'La Maledetta' badge on port fuselage side. White background to national markings in four wing positions; Bossi had to perform an emergency landing with this aircraft at Spa during the ferry flight from Italy to Belgium*

FIAT BR.20M Cicogna, *M.M.22250/5-2, 5ª Squadriglia, 43° Gruppo, 13° Stormo BT, CAI, Melsbroei (Belgium), November 1940. Giallo Mimetico 3, Verde Mimetico 3 and Marrone Mimetico 2 upper surfaces with Grigio Mimetico undersides. Codes in black and red; 'La Maledetta' badge on port fusALage side only. '2' in red on nose within a black 'teardrop'. Black fasces wing markings on a white background above and below the wings*

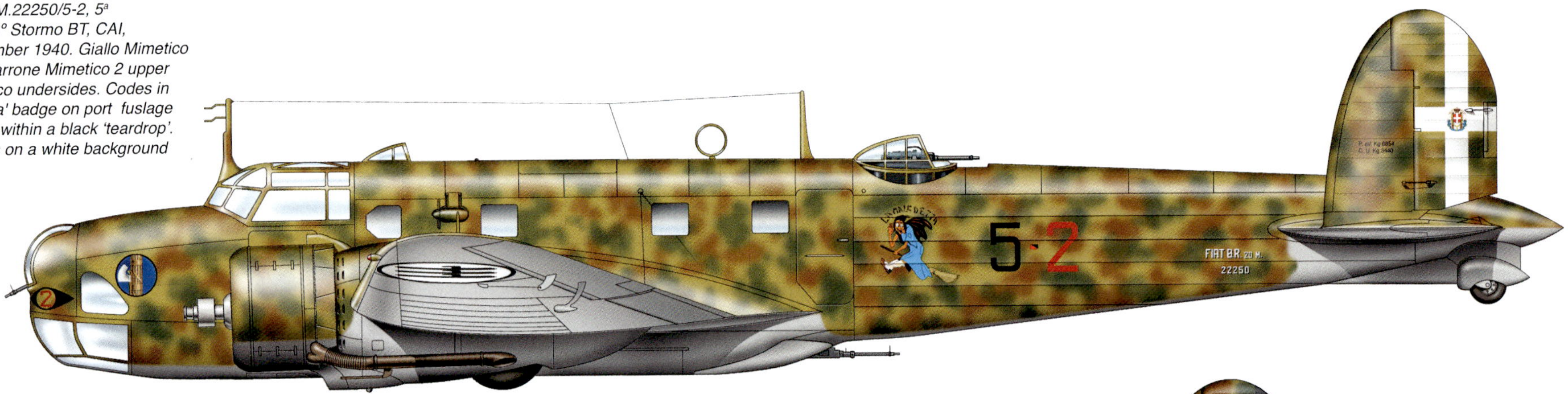

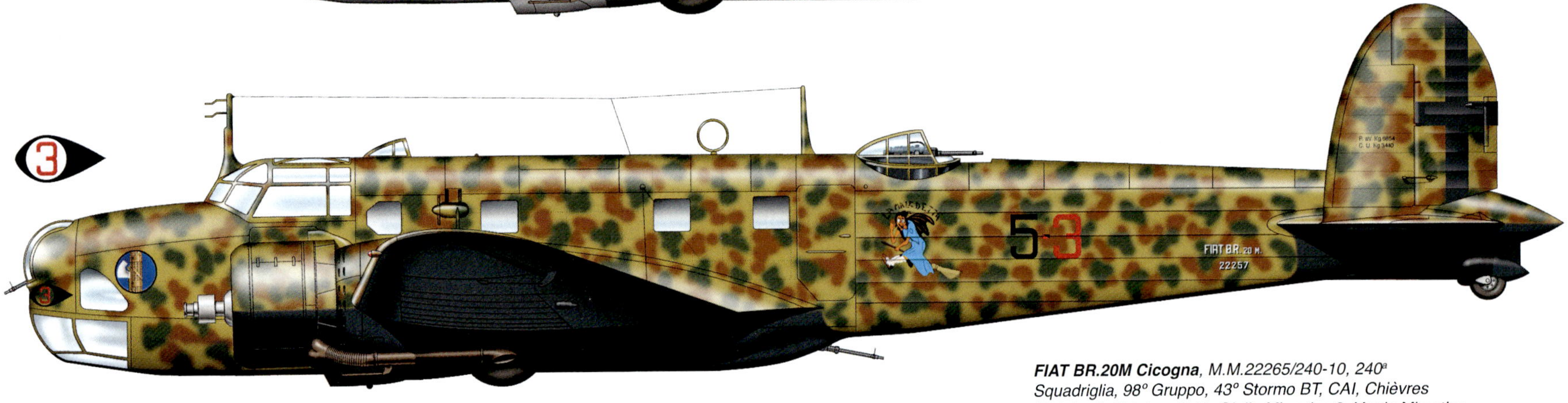

Above: FIAT BR.20M Cicogna, *M.M.22257/5-3, 5ª Squadriglia, 43° Gruppo, 13° Stormo BT, CAI, Melsbroei (Belgium), November 1940. Giallo Mimetico 3, Verde Mimetico 3 and Marrone Mimetico 2 upper surfaces with undersides and rudder cross marking overpainted in RLM22 (black). Codes in black and red; Black fasces wing markings on a white background above the wings. 'La Maledetta' badge on port fuslage side. '3' in red on nose within a black 'teardrop'.*

FIAT BR.20M Cicogna, *M.M.22265/240-10, 240ª Squadriglia, 98° Gruppo, 43° Stormo BT, CAI, Chièvres (Belgium), October 1940. Giallo Mimetico 3, Verde Mimetico 3 and Marrone Mimetico 2 upper surfaces with Grigio Mimetico undersides. Codes in black and red. Black fasces wing markings on a white background above and below the*

***FIAT BR.20M Cicogna**, M.M.21903/242-2, 242ª Squadriglia, 99° Gruppo, 43° Stormo BT, CAI, Chièvres (Belgium), November 1940. Giallo Mimetico 3, Verde Mimetico 3 and Marrone Mimetico 2 upper surfaces with undersides oversprayed in RLM 22 (black). Codes in black and red, with '2' repeared on nose. Serial in white with black drop shadow. National fasces markings in black over a white background above wings only*

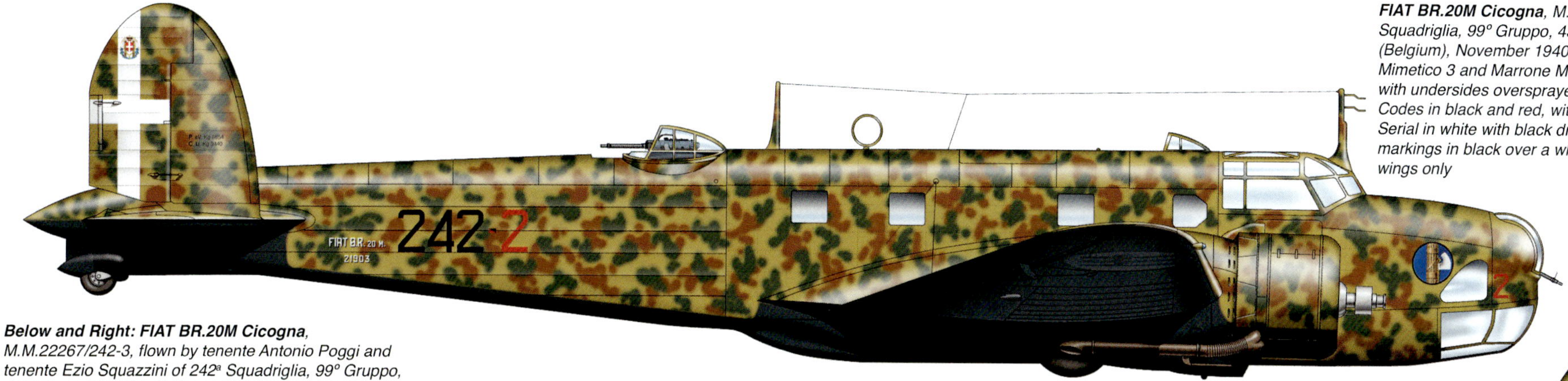

***Below and Right: FIAT BR.20M Cicogna**, M.M.22267/242-3, flown by tenente Antonio Poggi and tenente Ezio Squazzini of 242ª Squadriglia, 99° Gruppo, 43° Stormo BT, CAI, Chièvres (Belgium), October 1940. Giallo Mimetico 3, Verde Mimetico 3 and Marrone Mimetico 2 upper surfaces with Grigio Mimetico undersides; Giallo Cromo mid-fuselage band. Codes in black and red, serial in white; '3' repeated in white on nose. White backing to national markings in black in four wing positions*

***Below: FIAT BR.20M Cicogna**, M.M.21907/242-5, flown by capitano Nicola Volpe, 242ª Squadriglia, 99° Gruppo, 43° Stormo BT, Chièvres (Belgium), on the raid late 1940. Giallo Mimetico 3, Verde Mimetico 3 and Marrone Mimetico 2 upper surfaces with undersides oversprayed in RLM 22 (black). Fasces below the wing were partially overpainted white the white rudder crosses were full overpainted in black. Giallo Cromo mid-fuselage band. Codes in black and red, serial in white; '5' repeated in red on nose. White backing to national markings remained above the wings. One of only two BR.20s from 10 that managed to return to base from the day raid of 11 November 1940 and subsequently its finish was toned down as shown for night operations. Of the others, one tuned back due to engine trouble, three were shot down and the other four had to divert to other airfields in Belgium for landing*

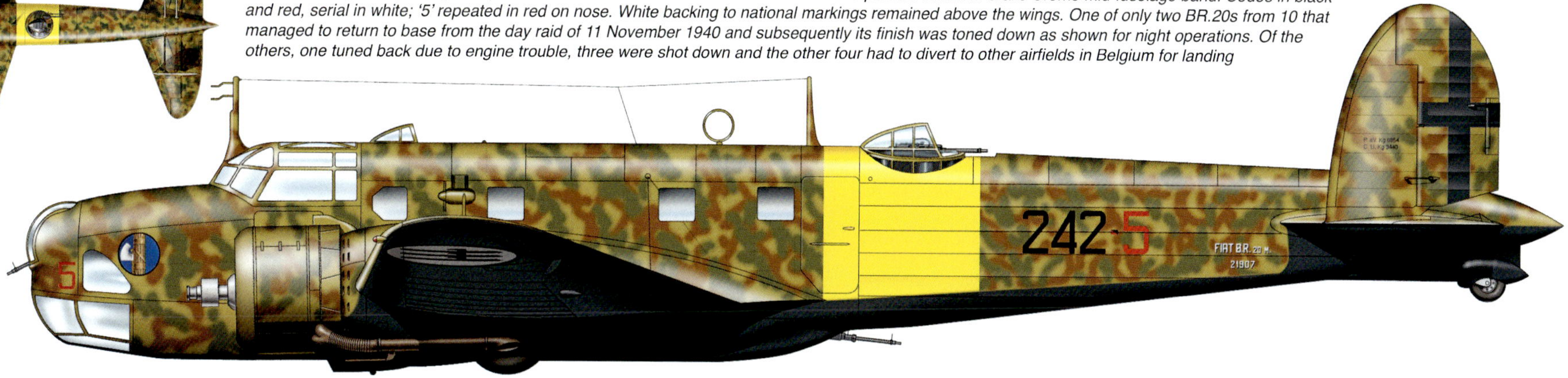

FIAT BR.20M Cicogna, *M.M.22621/243-2, flown by sottotenente Pietro Appiani and sergente pilota Giuliano Rigolone of 243ª Squadriglia, 99° Gruppo, 43° Stormo BT, CAI, based at Chièvres (Belgium), 1940. Giallo Mimetico 3, Verde Mimetico 3 and Marrone Mimetico 2 upper surfaces with Grigio Mimetico undersides. Codes in black and red, serial in white with black drop shadow. '2' repeated in white on nose. White backing to national markings in four wing positions. Shot down and crash landed in Tangham Forest, Bromswell, near Woodbridge. Radio-operator 1° aviere Armando Paolini had been killed in the air. Co-pilot Rigolone and flight engineer 1° avieri motorista Emmanuelle De Gasperi were wounded (Rigolone later died of his wounds); pilot sottotenente Appiani, 1° aviere motorista Degasperi and the unit's photographer avieri scelto Mario Pensa were taken prisoner. The sixth crew member 1° aviere Elvino Cerrosi (front air gunner and bombardier), survived unhurt and was also taken prisoner*

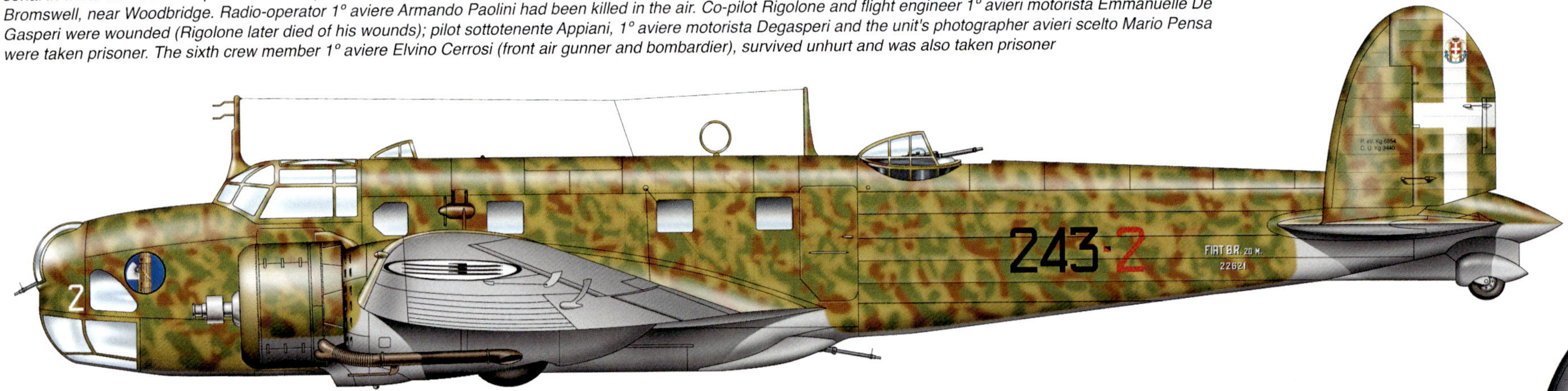

FIAT BR.20M Cicogna, *M.M.21907/242-5, flown by capitano Nicola Volpe, 242ª Squadriglia, 99° Gruppo, 43° Stormo BT, CAI, Chièvres (Belgium), on the raid late 1940. Giallo Mimetico 3, Verde Mimetico 3 and Marrone Mimetico 2 upper surfaces with undersides, fuselage sides and vertical tail surfaces over-sprayed in RLM 22 (black).*

FIAT BR.20M Cicogna, *A second version of RLM 22 application on the undersides, with most of the fuselage camouflage being overpainted to a high line above the side windows. When the 'night' finish was applied, all identity markings were overpainted. Black national fasces markings on a white background were retained above the wings*

Caproni Ca.133T. *85CT, 85ª Squadriglia, 20° Gruppo, 56° Stormo, CAI, Ursel (Belgium), October 1940. Giallo Mimetico 3, Verde Mimetico 3 and Marrone Mimetico 2 upper surfaces with Grigio Mimetico undersides; Blue-grey codes with black drop shadow. White background to national markings above the wings, reversed below with black background and white markings*

Caproni Ca.133T. *352ª Squadriglia, 20° Gruppo, 56° Stormo, CAI, Maldegem (Belgium), October 1940. Giallo Mimetico 3, Verde Mimetico 3 and Marrone Mimetico 2 upper surfaces with Grigio Mimetico undersides; Giallo Cromo band around fuselage. White background to wing markings above wings, reversed black on white below wings; 51° Gruppo 'cat & mice' badge on fin (both sides)*

ORDER OF BATTLE: Corpo Aereo Italiano

13° Stormo Bombardemento Terrestre			
11° Gruppo Bombardamento Terrestre	1ª, 4ª Squadriglie	10 FIAT BR.20M	Melsbroek
43° Gruppo Bombardamento Terrestre	3ª, 5ª Squadriglie	10 FIAT BR.20M	Melsbroek
43° Stormo Bombardemento Terrestre			
98° Gruppo Bombardamento Terrestre	240ª, 241ª Squadriglie	10 FIAT BR.20M	Chièvres
99° Gruppo Bombardemento Terrestre	242ª, 243ª Squadriglie	10 FIAT BR.20M	Chièvres
56° Stormo Caccia Terrestre			
18° Caccia Terrestre	83ª, 85ª, 95ª Squadriglie	50 FIAT CR42	Maldegem
20° Caccia Terrestre	351ª, 352ª, 353ª Squadriglie	45 FIAT G.50	Maldegem
	172ª Squadriglia Ricognizione Strategica	5 CANT Z.1007	Chièvres

History

The Regia Aeronautica on the Russian Front

On 22 June 1941 Germany launched OPERATION BARBAROSSA, the invasion of Russia, an offensive planned similar to those that had swept over Western Europe, the well-proven *Blitzkrieg*. As Italy joined other Axis forces in declaring war against the Soviet Union, Benito Mussolini also decided to dispatch a land expeditionary force, the *Corpo di Spedizione dell'Esercito* (CSIR) supported by a rectively small air component. Such a decision deprived the *Regia Aeronautica* of much needed aircraft, spares, fuel and all other supporting crews much more needed on other fronts, particularly Malta and North Africa. Not forgetting the bitter taste left by the operations of the first CAI during the Battle of Britain.

The Luftwaffe threw more than half of its aircraft into battle on the Russian Front, consisting of close to 2,770 combat aircraft, including 775 bombers, 310 dive bombers, 830 single seat fighters, 90 two seat fighters, 710 reconnaissance and 55 coastal patrol aircraft.

Italy could only put together a much smaller force, made up of 85 fighters, bombers, reconnaissance and transport aircraft. A signal dated 5 August 1941 received by the *Ufficio Operazioni del Comando* of Italian forces in Albania from *generale* Ferruccio Ranza ordered the move of the 22° *Gruppo Caccia Terrestre* (CT) equipped with Macchi C.200s, the 38° *Stormo* with their FIAT BR.20s, to be followed by the three Caproni Ca.133s of the 22° *Gruppo* CT and two Savoia Marchetti S.81s that were also attached to the 22° *Gruppo* CT.

An advance party of ground support personnel from the 22° *Gruppo* left Tirana by sea to Bari from where they continued by train to Vigodarzere and on to Tudora in Romania. Commander of air forces in Russia *colonello* Carlo Drago flew on a S.75 to

Tirana to co-ordinate operations with *generale* Ferruccio Ranza, commander of air forces in Albania, and then on to Mostar, base of the 61° *Gruppo*. He then proceeded to Belgrade, Bucharest and finally Tudora for the same purpose.

Defending the Soviet Union in the air was the responsibility of the *Voenno-Vozdushnye Sily Soyuza Sovetskih Sotsialisticheskih Respublik* (VVS SSSR), which translates as Military Air Forces of the Union of Soviet Socialist Republics (hereafter referred to as VVS). It had some 11-12,000 aircraft on strength at the time of the German invasion, of which less than 3,000 could be considered to be modern, mainly consisting of the Yak-1, MiG-3 (the most numerous of the fighter element), LaGG-3, Il-2 and Pe-2. During the first few days the high losses of the VVS were mainly suffered on the ground, while those in the air were mainly due to the inexperience of its pilots.

The Macchi C.200 Saetta

In the hands of an expert fighter pilot the C.200 *Saetta* could prove to be a match for any opponent notwithstanding the 'aged' look of its bulky radial engine and open cockpit. Born at a time when fighter aircraft were going through a fast phase of development, it was soon overtaken by aircraft with more sophisticated features. The C.200, however, proved to be a very sensible design which eventually gave birth to the all-time classic, the C.202 Folgore, followed by the finest piston engined aircraft ever designed in Italy, the C.205 Veltro.

In July 1935, the *Regia Aeronautica* issued a call for the design and production of a new type of fighter aircraft then considered to feature contemporary standards. The new fighter was required to be powered by an air-cooled radial engine, be armed with two 12.7mm machine guns and one 20mm

Facing Page: Macchi C.200s of the 386ª Squadriglia during summer of 1941. Note two different style of camouflage application

Below: Macchi C.200 Saettas of the 369ª Squadriglia parked on the snow covered Stalino airfield in February 1942. Their colour scheme is far from ideal for the terrain they operated on and there was no effort to tone down the bright camouflage colours

A Macchi C.200 fitted with wing mounted cine cameras on the leading edge of the wings This is probably one of the three such flown to Russia by Capitano Carlo Maurizio Ruspoli's, Reparto Cinematografico di Volo, 22° Gruppo for propaganda filming purposes. These Macchis were left behind in Russia afterwards to boost the force of 21° Gruppo C.200s

cannon. The possibility of an additional rôle, such as ground attack, was also to be considered.

By early the following year cannon armament and external bomb-racks were deleted from the specification to cut down on overall weight. As no in-line engine of the necessary power was available in Italy at the time its designer, Mario Castoldi, opted for the bulky Fiat A.74 RC.38 which provided 840hp at 3,800m driving a variable pitch, three-bladed metal propeller. The all-metal construction was a massive step forward in the aviation construction industry at that time.

Flight trials were originally the responsibility of Giuseppe Burei who took the C.200 prototype (MM336) up for its first flight on Christmas Eve of 1937 at Lonate Pozzolo (Varese). Ambrogio Colombo took over the flight test programme for a short while when Burei was killed testing the twin-engined Macchi C.94. Spanish war veteran Adriano Mantelli was handed over the testing of the C.200 in June 1938.

By Italy's entry into World War II on 10 June 1940 Macchi had delivered 99 examples. The all-round vision cockpit hood was greatly disliked by pilots accustomed to the open cockpits of biplanes so the canopy was replaced with an open cockpit arrangement.

First deliveries of the C.200, now named *Saetta*, went to the 10° *Gruppo* of the 4° *Stormo* in the autumn of 1939. This unit soon passed its aircraft to the 6° *Gruppo* of the 1° *Stormo* in exchange to the CR.42 biplane. At the outbreak of war the C.200 was operational with the 153° *Gruppo* at Vergiate, the 152° *Gruppo* at Airasca and the 6° *Gruppo* at Catania, in Sicily. The latter was the first unit to go into real action on the morning of 11 June 1940 opening the aerial combat over Malta.

The second operational front for the C.200 was North Africa where the first examples arrived in April of 1941 with the 143ª *Squadriglia*, followed by the 153° *Gruppo* in July. By summer of 1942 aircraft from the 18° *Gruppo* of the 3° *Stormo* were fitted with underwing bomb racks earning the name of *Bombe Alari* -Flying Bombs').

Early in the morning of 9 August 1941 the 51 Macchi C.200s of the 22° *Gruppo* left Tirana, staged through Belgrade and arrived in Bucharest flying in a perfect tight formation at low level over Vanessa airfield and landing all together under torrential rain. None of the requirements agreed with *colonello* Drago were in place and personnel had to be billeted in temporary conditions. Bad weather forced the unit to remain at Bucharest for some days during which time the C.200s' rear fuselage band and underside of the wingtips were painted yellow using paint supplied by the *Luftwaffe*. As weather conditions improved, the 22° *Gruppo* could leave Bucharest for Tudora staging through Roman. The airfield had up to some time earlier a cultivated field and the surface was so rough that a number of C.200s suffered tailwheel damage which required a couple of days to repair. On 26 August the unit left for their final destination of Krivoi-Rog.

The following day the 22° *Gruppo* was already in action, as 27 C.200s in three formations intercepted a formation of Tupolev SB-2 *Katjuscia* bombers escorted by Polikarpov I-16 *Rata* fighters, both types veteran Italian pilots had previously encountered over Spain during the Civil War. During the encounter six Soviet bombers and two fighters were shot down without suffering any losses. Giovanni Bonet, Giovanni Cervellin, Mario Longoni, Marcello Baracca, Rodolfo Stoppani and Attilio Sanson were among the pilots that scored victories that day. This initial success was greeted with such enthusiasm within the *Regia Aeronautica* that *generale* Pircolo, *Capo di Stato Maggiore Aeronautica Militare* (Chief of the Air Force General Staff) sent a telegram of congratulations to the unit.

In the afternoon of 28 August eleven C.200s of the 362ª *Squadriglia* under the command of *capitano* Germano La Ferla were requested to support a German advanced column, returning to base a couple of hours later without engaging the enemy. During the landing sequence *tenente pilota* Mario Longoni's C.200 spun into the ground due to a technical problem as it approached the airfield. He was the first Italian to lose his life on the Russian Front; his remains were only returned to Italy in September 2009.

At the end of August the C.200s moved to Kryvyi Rih in the south of Ukraine and towards the end of September was operating from Zaporižžja in the south-east Another move saw the 371ª *Squadriglia* move to Donec'k. After months of losing ground and considerable war material, the Soviets launched a counter-offensive on Christmas Eve of 1941 forcing Italian ground troops to retreat under the difficult aerial support of the C.200s that strafed and attacked using 50kg bombs the Soviet advanced ground forces. The Macchis also had to control as best they could the Soviet bombers and fighters supporting the counter offensive.

By the end of the year the C.200s had 12 aerial victories to their credit against the loss of only one Italian fighter. Fierce fighting continued into the new year, as the C.200s strafed the enemy airfield of Kranyl where they destroyed 10 aircraft on the ground and another five in the air without any loss. The aircraft was certainly not suited for this type of environment – ground crew had to work in the open at -30° while pilots had to fly in open cockpits. Heated flying suits of German origin were provided but these proved to be either defective or ineffective.

This was the pattern of operations by the 22° *Gruppo* over the next months adding four aerial victories during February and a further 14 in March. The unit's operational cycle on the Russian Front came to an end on 4 May 1942 when the 22° *Gruppo* left for home, leaving their aircraft to be taken over by the personnel of the 21° *Gruppo*. By that time, the 22° *Gruppo* had scored 88 victories for the loss of 15 C.200s

The 21° Gruppo did not have the opportunity to share its predecessor's successes as it was by then engaged in defending the retreat of the Italian and German ground forces along the 1000 kms won the previous summer.

Enter the Macchi C.202

The Russian front saw the deployment of a small number of Macchi C.202s. By July 1942 the 22° *Gruppo* reached its operational limit and was replaced by the 21° *Gruppo* composed of the 356ª, 365ª, 382ª and 386ª *Squadriglie* equipped with new C.200s.

In September 1942, twelve examples were distributed among the four units of the 21° *Gruppo* that at the time were still flying the older C.200. Their operations commenced in November, just before the Soviet counter-offensive that was launched on the 19th of that month.

Among other missions, the C.202s were required to perform fighter escort to the Italian bombers, primarily Fiat BR.20Ms and Caproni Ca.311s attacking Soviet Army columns. At times even Cant Z.1007bis flying reconnaissance missions had to be escorted. Although the C.202 could hold its own against most of the older Soviet Air Force fighters, the new generation of fighter aircraft appearing on the Russian Front, together with their increasing numbers, caused Italian losses to escalate.

Advanced airfields from where the Italian Corps was operating had be abandoned between December 1942 and January 1943 and had to assume a more defensive role. In March the units moved to Odessa, a base they shared

Two views showing the typical Italian Marus flying suit combination which with internal removeable padding could be used both in winter and in summer. The 382ª Squadriglia pilot on the left wears also the standard issue Salvator parachute used by Regia Aeronautica pilots. The 21° Gruppo pilot below must feel quiite lucky to have made it back to base with such battle damage to the wing of his Macchi C.200

One of the twelve Macchi C.202s pressed into service with the 21° Gruppo Autonomo. This must be one of three allocated to the 382ª Squadriglia which operated from Voroscilovgrad in September 1942. So obvious is the unsuitable colour scheme designed for operations in North Africa

with Hungarian Re.2000s Heja I and Romanian IAR 80Cs and Bf 109s. The final sortie for the *Regia Aeronuatica*'s Macchi C.202s over Soviet territory was flown on 17 January 1943 when a mixed formation of 25 surviving C.200s and C.202s attacked Red Army armoured and motorised infantry columns to support German and Italian units on the ground encircled in Millerovo. This marked a tragic end to a badly planned operation, which saw the Folgore being sent unprepared and in too small numbers in such precarious conditions, such as having to operate in temperatures well minus 40° C from snow-covered airfields.

Bombers and Transports

The 61° *Gruppo* arrived at Otipeni (Bucharest) on 11 August 1941 after staging through Belgrade. The aerial observation unit was composed of the 34ª, 119ª and 128ª *Squadriglie* flying the Caproni Ca.311 and had the support of a single Savoia-Marchetti S.82.The 34ª *Squdriglia* moved to Krivoi Rog while the 128ª took up base at Stalino towards the end of October. Apart from their usual role the Ca.311s also performed light bombing duties and by Spring of the following year the 61° was replaced by the 71° *Gruppo* with its 38ª and 116ª *Squadriglie* providing support to the handful of FIAT BR. 20 bombers in the Voroscilovgrad zone.

Early the following Spring the unit withdrew to Saporoshje, and soon later to Odessa. Attrition was such that by April 1943 the 71° *Gruppo* either destroyed or rendered thier aircraft unserviceable. Another Caproni type operated in Russia consisted of three Ca.133T (T-Transport) and a single Ca.133S (S- Sanitario, air ambulance) allocated to the 247ª *Squadriglia*; the 38ª and 116ª *Squadriglie* equipped with BR.20Ms were each provided with a Ca.113S which were at times considered to be medically better equipped that their counterparts on the ground.

An initial batch of three BR.20Ms from the 38ª *Squadriglia* arrived in Russia on 3 August 1942. This unit belonged to the 71° *Gruppo Osservazione Aerea* (Air Observation Group) in support of the Caproni Ca.311s. On 5 September they were joined by three more from the 43° *Stormo*. Five more aircraft were supplied on 9 December so that all the BR.20Ms could be formed into two *Squadriglie*, the 38ª and 116ª at Odessa.

The severe Russian winter forced these aircraft to fly, on several occasions with undercarriage and guns completely frozen and inoperable. By 11 December, the massive Soviet counter-offensive had reached the Italian-held sector, and after a week of fierce fighting the Axis lines had been penetrated. This marked the beginning of a catastrophic retreat, during which the 71° *Gruppo* was reduced to a mere shadow, returning home on 13 april 1943 with six surviving BR.20Ms,

All the above units required a link with Italy for the transportation of material and personnel. For this reason the *Sezione Trasporti Aviazione* CSIR (Air Transport Section) was formed on 1 September 1941 at Bucharest, on four S.81s taken from the 56° *Gruppo* (18° *Stormo*). Eight more aircraft were added to the unit which was designated 245ª *Squadriglia*, while the 246ª was added soon after based at Saporoshje and a third, the 247ª, was added in Januaary 1942.

Apart from keeping the flying units well supplied these aircraft were also asked to bring aid to some ground units that had found themselves encircled or cut off from the main force such as at Certkowo in December 1942. On the return flight to its base at Woroschilowgrad, after having unloaded food and other supplies, the S.81 from the 245ª *Squadriglia* (MM 20942) was lost, later ascertained to have crashed behind enemy lines. On board that flight was *generale* Enrico Pezzi who had decided to go and verify the situation at Certkowo in person.Italy's entry into the Second World War, declared on 10 June 1940, was a miscalculated and misguided attempt at grabbing part of the loot that would otherwise have ended up completely in the hands of the fast conquering German war machine. Following a short and ineffective cycle of operations against France it had already become apparent that Italy was ill-equipped for a modern war and lacked a clear strategy and plan of action.

Only eleven FIAT BR.20Ms were sent to Russia. These belonged to two Squadriglie of the 71° Gruppo Osservazione Aerea, the 38ª and 116ª. Operations in the severe winter of 1942-43 restricted their use and only six managed to return to Italy in spring of 1943.

Colour Art - Russian Front

Aer Macchi C.200 Saetta, *362-1, 362ª Squadriglia, 22° Gr Autonomo Caccia Terrestre (C.T.), Krivoirog (Russia), summer 1941. Verde Mimetico upper surfaces with Giallo and Marrone Mimetico mottling; Grigio Mimetico undersides. Yellow engine cowling, fuselage band and below outer sections of wings; white triangles above and below wings. Code in black and white; unit badge on forward fuselage. Black outline markings above wings; white markings on a black background below wings*

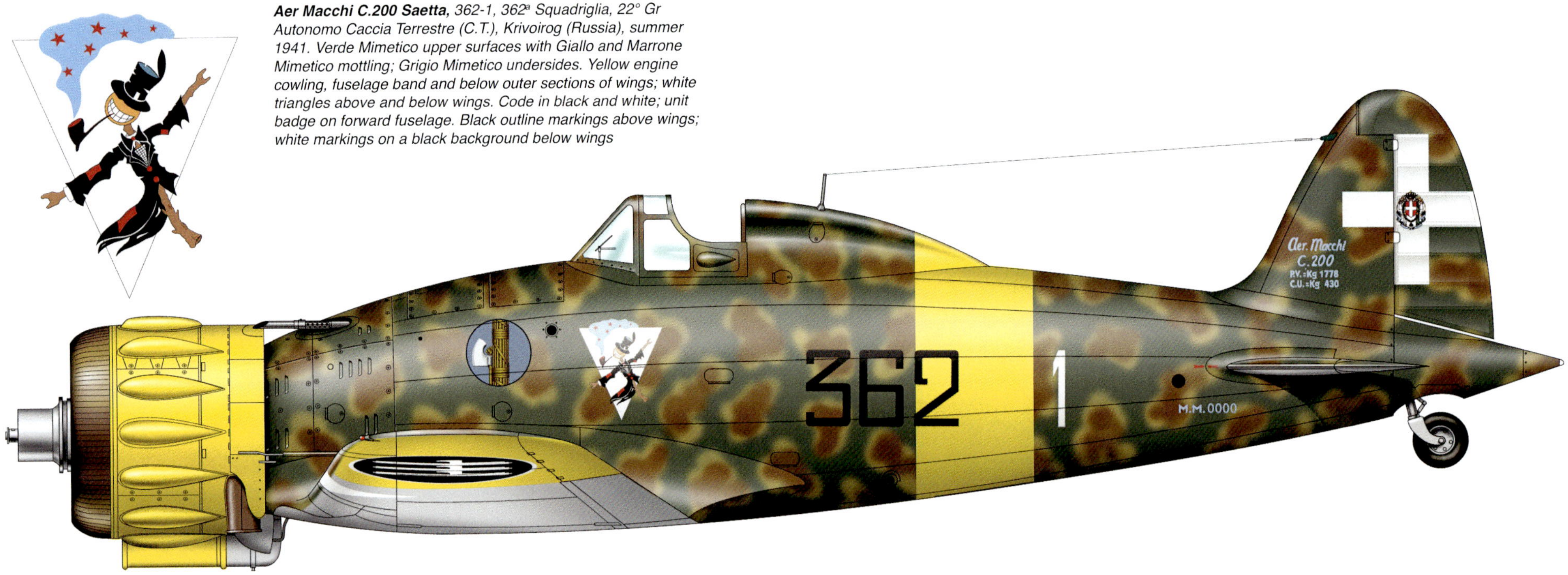

Aer Macchi C.200 Saetta, *359-4, 359ª Squadriglia, 22° Gruppo Autonomo C.T., Regia Aeronautica, Tudora (Romania), summer 1941. Verde Mimetico upper surfaces with mottling of Giallo Mimetico and Marrone Mimetico; Grigio Mimetico undersides. Yellow engine cowling, fuselage band and below outer sections of wings; white triangles above and below wings. Codes are black and red, with '4' having a white drop shadow*

***Aer Macchi C.200 Saetta,** 359-8, 359ª Squadriglia, 22º Gruppo Autonomo C.T., Regia Aeronautica, Tudora (Romania), summer 1941. Verde Mimetico upper surfaces with mottling of Giallo Mimetico and Marrone Mimetico; Grigio Mimetico undersides. Yellow engine cowling, fuselage band and below outer sections of wings; white triangles above and below wings. Codes are black and red*

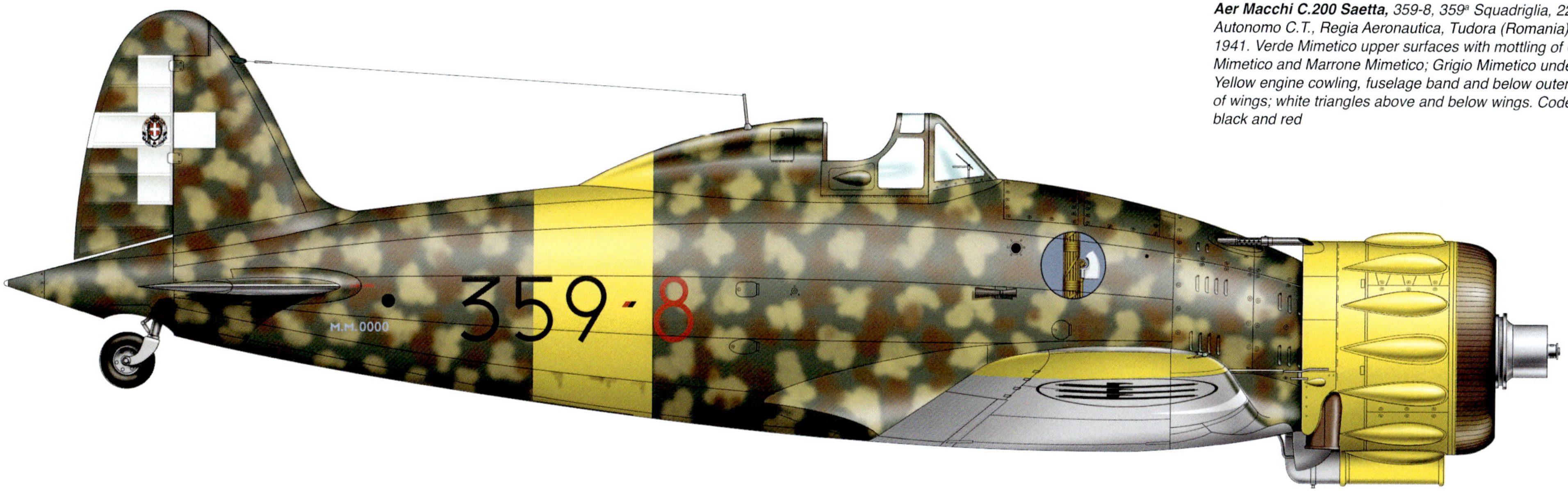

***Aer Macchi C.200 Saetta,** 371-11, 371ª Squadriglia, 22º Gruppo Autonomo C.T., Regia Aeronautica, Tudora (Rokmania), summer 1941. Verde Mimetico upper surfaces with Giallo and Marrone Mimetico mottling; Grigio Mimetico undersides. Giallo Cromo fuselage band and below outer sections of wings; white triangles above and below wings. Code in black and red. Note heavy weathering on fuselage band and the absence of the left arm of the white cross on the tail*

Aer Macchi C.200 Saetta, *362-2, 362ª Squadriglia, 22° Gruppo Autonomo C.T., Regia Aeronautica, August 1941. Verde Mimetico upper surfaces with Giallo and Marrone Mimetico mottling; Grigio Mimetico undersides. Yellow engine cowling, fuselage band and below outer sections of wings; white triangles above and below wings. Code in black. Note non-standard proportions of tail cross*

Aer Macchi C.200 Saetta, *359-1, flown by capitano pilota Vittorio Minguzzi, Commander of 359ª Squadriglia, 22° Gruppo Autonomo C.T., Regia Aeronautica, Tudora (Romania), August 1941. Verde Mimetico upper surfaces with Giallo and Marrone Mimetico mottling; Grigio Mimetico undersides. Yellow fuselage band and below outer sections of wings; white triangles above and below wings. Roundels below the wings in black with white outline and fasces. Codes in black and red. Note replacement unpainted tail cone*

Aer Macchi C.200 Saetta, *371-12, 371ª Squadriglia, 22° Gruppo Autonomo C.T., Regia Aeronautica, Tudora (Romania), August 1941. Verde Mimetico upper surfaces with Giallo and Marrone Mimetico mottling; Grigio Mimetico undersides. Yellow fuselage band and below outer sections of wings; white triangles above and below wings. Code in black and red*
Note: that red codes were discouraged and most were repainted in black or white, to avoid being mistaken for the Soviet star on the fuselage of enemy aircraft

Aer Macchi C.200 Saetta, *'22', flown by maggiore pilota Giovanni Borzoni, Commander of the 22° Gruppo Autonomo C.T., Regia Aeronautica, summer 1941. Verde Mimetico upper surfaces with Giallo and Marrone Mimetico mottling; Grigio Mimetico undersides. Yellow fuselage band and below outer sections of wings; white triangles above and below wings. Codes in black, with rank pennant in black on a white background aft of code '22'. White leading edges to all tail surfaces. Unit badge aft of fuselage band*

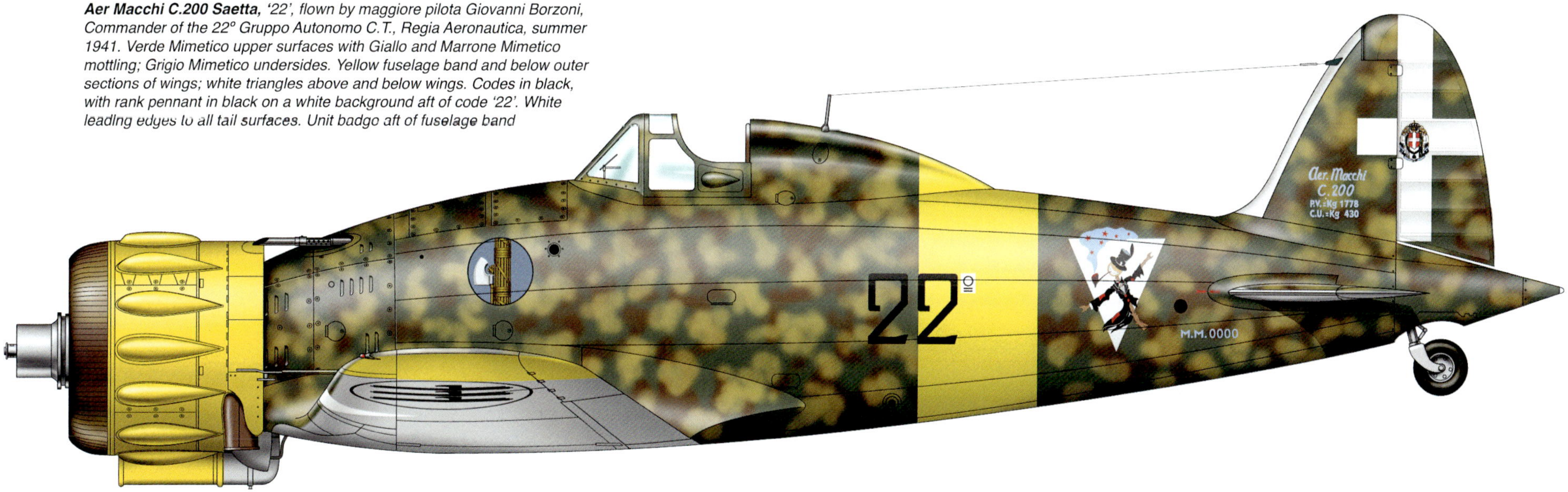

Aer Macchi C.200 Saetta, *359-5, 359ª Squadriglia, 22° Gruppo Autonomo C.T., Regia Aeronautica, Tudora (Romania), mid-August 1941. Verde Mimetico upper surfaces with mottling of Giallo Mimetico with Grigio Mimetico undersides. Yellow fuselage band and below outer sections of wings; white triangles above and below wings. Codes are black and red*

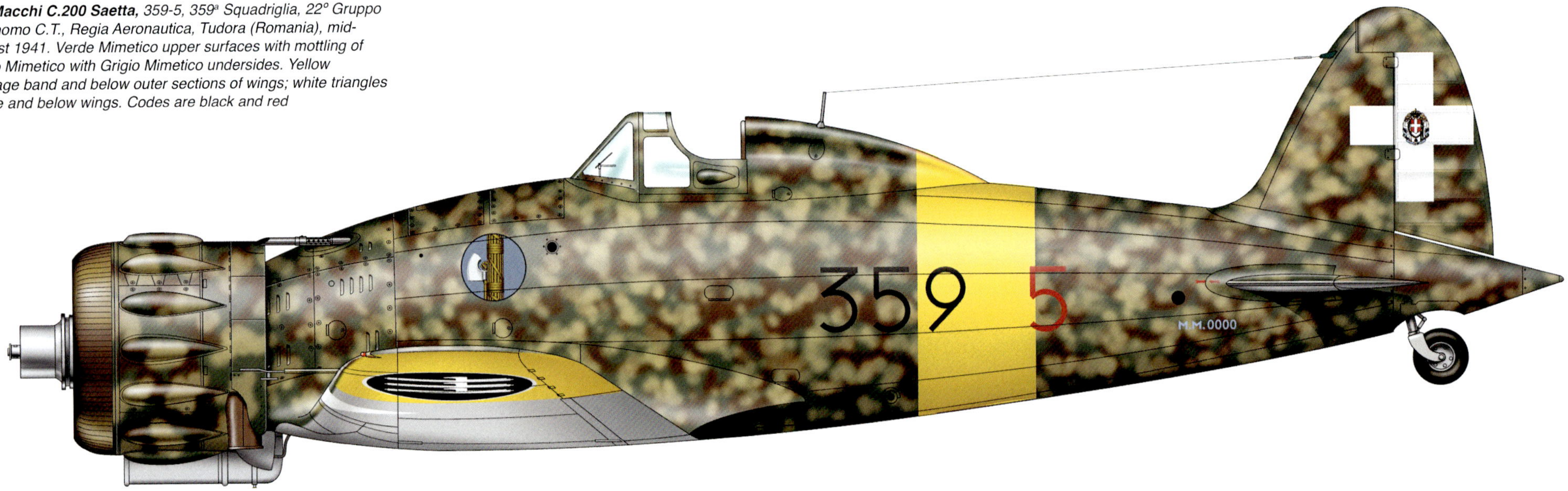

Aer Macchi C.200 Saetta, *362-4, 362ª Squadriglia, 22° GruppoAutonomo C.T., Russia, August 1941. Verde Mimetico upper surfaces with Giallo and Marrone Mimetico mottling; Grigio Mimetico undersides. Yellow engine cowling, fuselage band and below outer sections of wings; white triangles above and below wings. Code in black and white; unit badge on forward fuselage. Black outline markings above wings; white markings on a black background below wings*

Aer Macchi C.200 Saetta, *369-1 flown by maggiore pilota Borzoni of the 369ª Squadriglia, 22° Gruppo Autonomo CT, Stalino (Russia), September 1941. Verde Mimetico with Giallo and Marrone Mimetico 'poached egg' mottling on upper surfaces; Grigio Mimetico undersides. Yellow cowling, undersides of wingtips and rear fuselage band, with a norrow white band aft of the latter; codes in black and red. Unit badge, over a red patch, below windscreen (both sides). White triangles applied above and below wings at the leading edges*

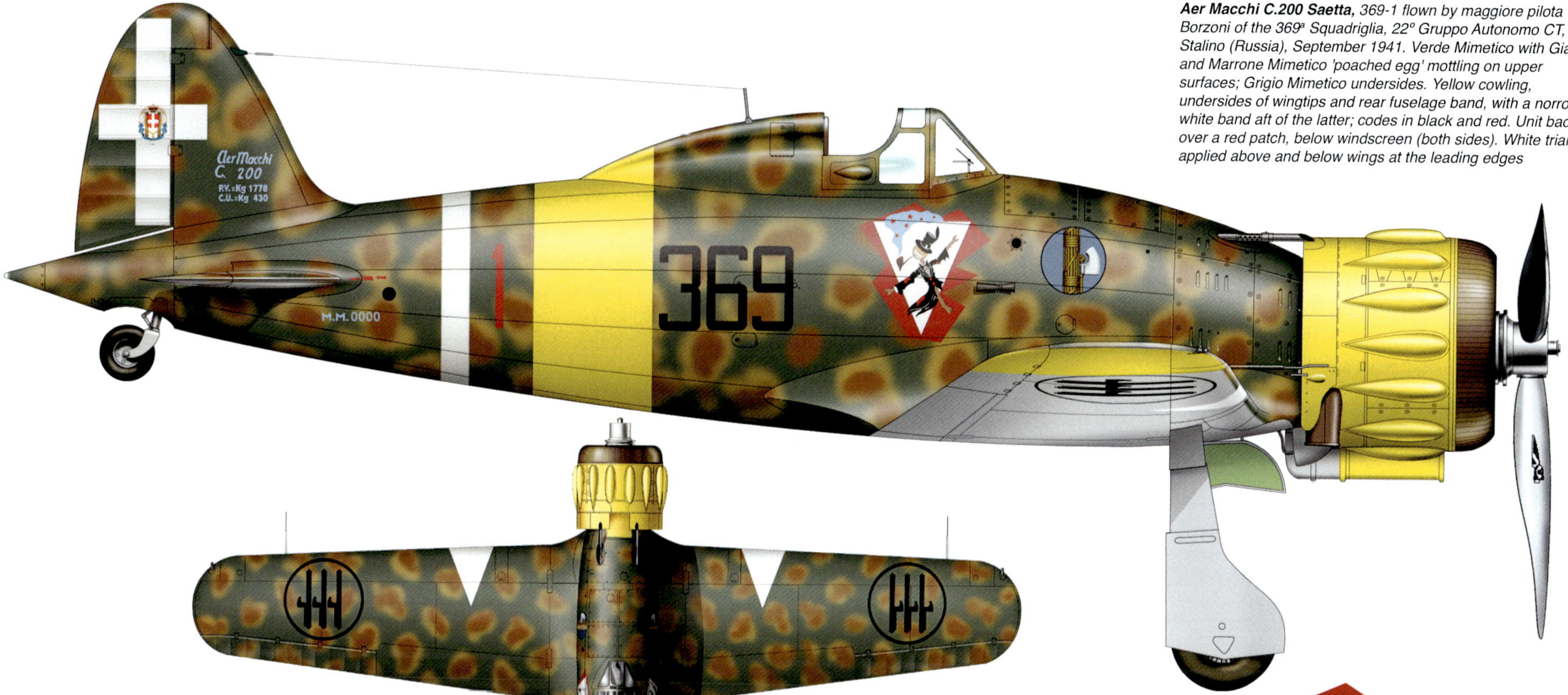

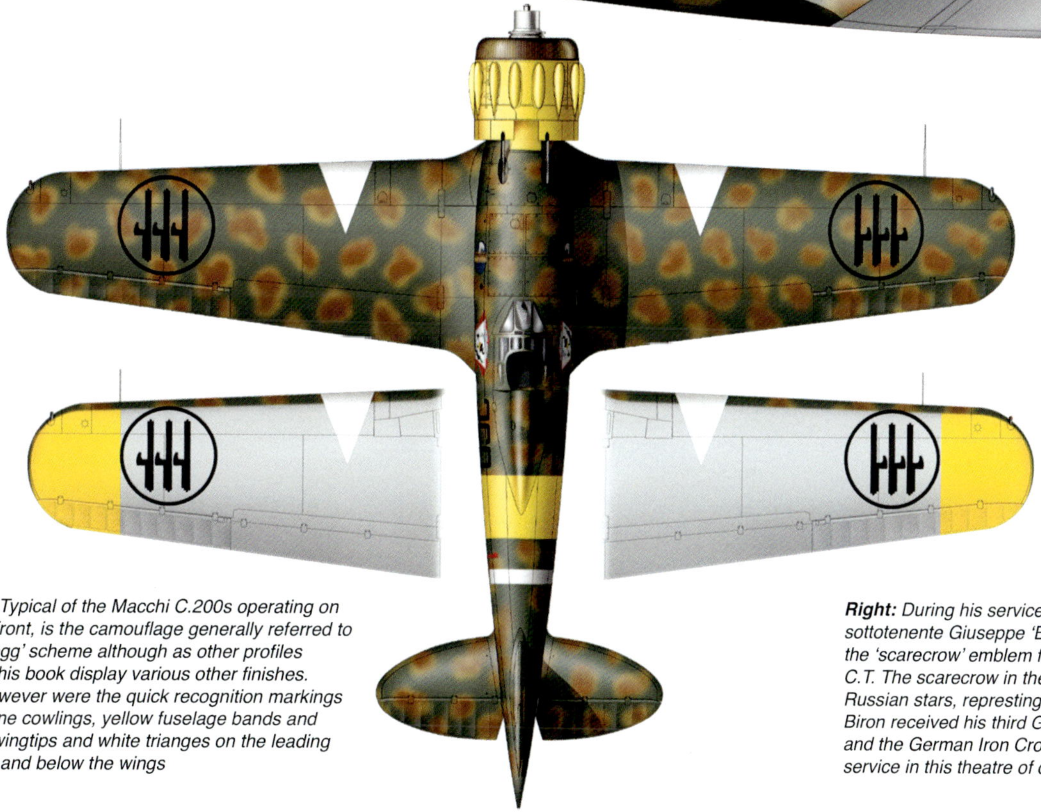

Above right: *Typical of the Macchi C.200s operating on the Russian Front, is the camouflage generally referred to as 'poached egg' scheme although as other profiles presented in this book display various other finishes. Mandatory however were the quick recognition markings of yellow engine cowlings, yellow fuselage bands and underside of wingtips and white trianges on the leading edges, above and below the wings*

Right: *During his service on the Russian Front sottotenente Giuseppe 'Bepi' Biron designed the 'scarecrow' emblem for the 22° Gruppo C.T. The scarecrow in the emblem is 'smoking' Russian stars, repesting enemy bombers. Biron received his third Gold Medal for Valour and the German Iron Cross II Class during his service in this theatre of operations*

Aer Macchi C.200 Saetta, *369-5, 369ª Squadriglia, 22° Gruppo Autonomo C.T. Regia Aeronautica, Stalino, December 1941. Verde Mimetico upper surfaces with Giallo and Marrone Mimetico mottling; Grigio Mimetico undersides. Yellow engine cowling, fuselage band and below outer sections of wings; white triangles above and below wings.Codes in black and white. White disc on aft fuselage and unit badge on forward fuselage*

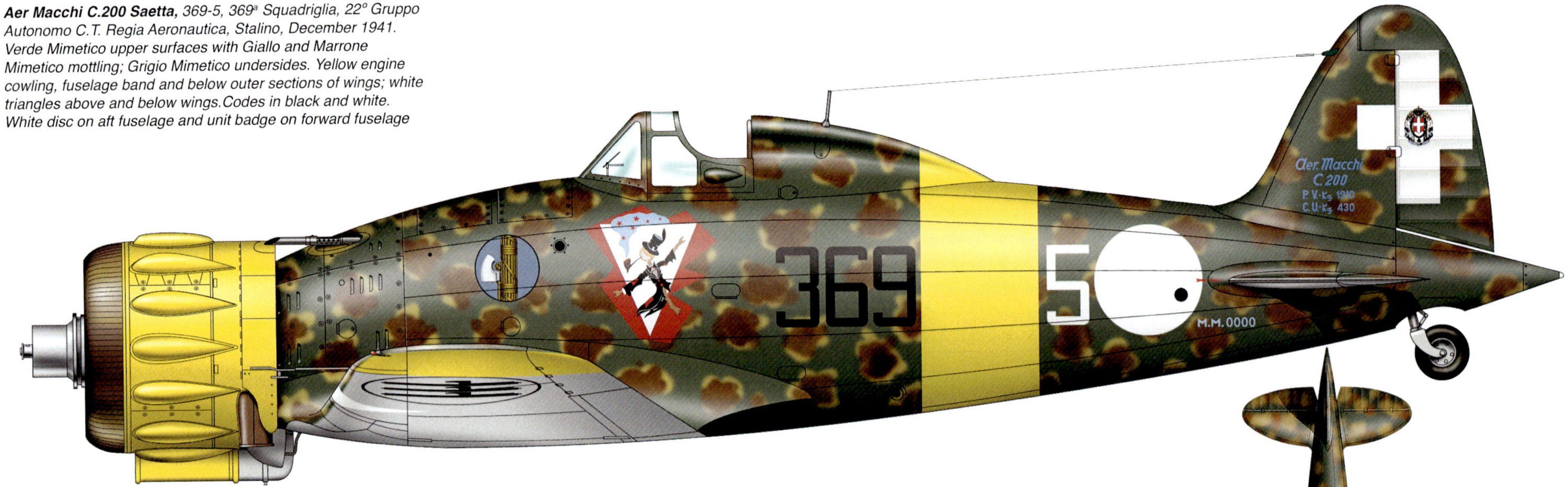

Aer Macchi C.200 Saetta, *362-3, 362ª Squadriglia, 22° Gruppo Autonomo C.T., Krivoi Rog (Russia), September 1941. Verde Mimetico upper surfaces with Giallo and Marrone Mimetico mottling; Grigio Mimetico undersides. Yellow engine cowling, and below outer sections of wings; white rear fuselage band, triangles above and below wings (note traingles added to wingtips (top only). Code in black and red*

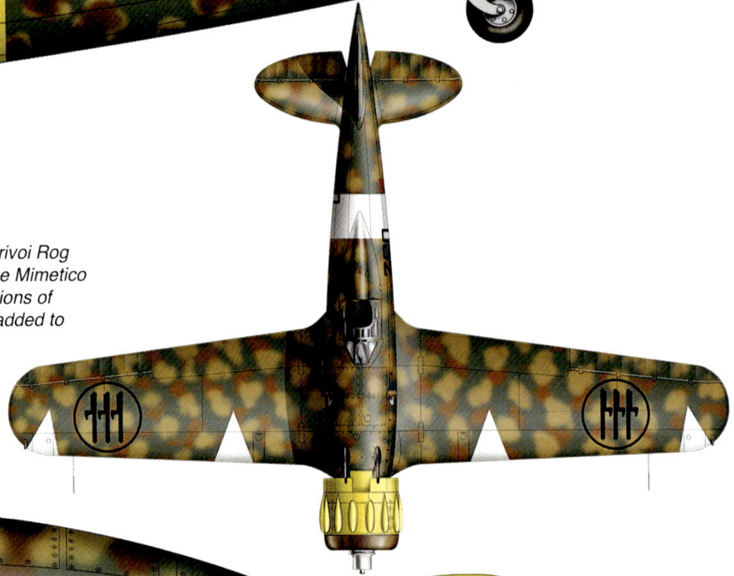

Aer Macchi C.200 Saetta, *369-3, flown by sottotenente Giuseppe 'Bepi' Biron, 369ª Squadriglia, 22º Gruppo Autonomo C.T., Stalino, February 1942. Verde Mimetico upper surfaces with mottling of Giallo Mimetico with Grigio Mimetico undersides. Yellow engine cowling, fuselage band and below outer sections of wings; white triangles above and below wings. Codes are all black. Unit badge on forward fuselage. Biron scored six victoies during his operations on the Russian Front*

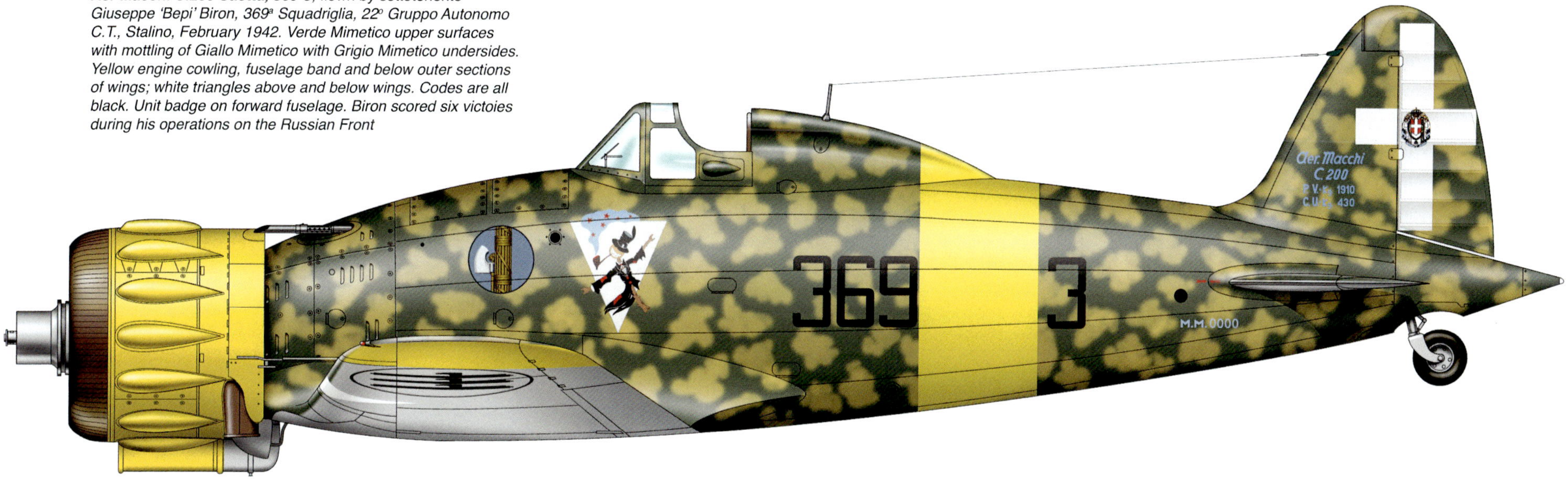

Aer Macchi C.200 Saetta, *386-4, 386ª Squadriglia, 21º Gruppo Autonomo C.T., Regia Aeronautica, Russian front, summer 1942. Verde Mimetico upper surfaces with Giallo and Marrone Mimetico mottling; Grigio Mimetico undersides. Yellow engine cowling, fuselage band and below outer sections of wings; white triangles above and below wings. Code in black and white*

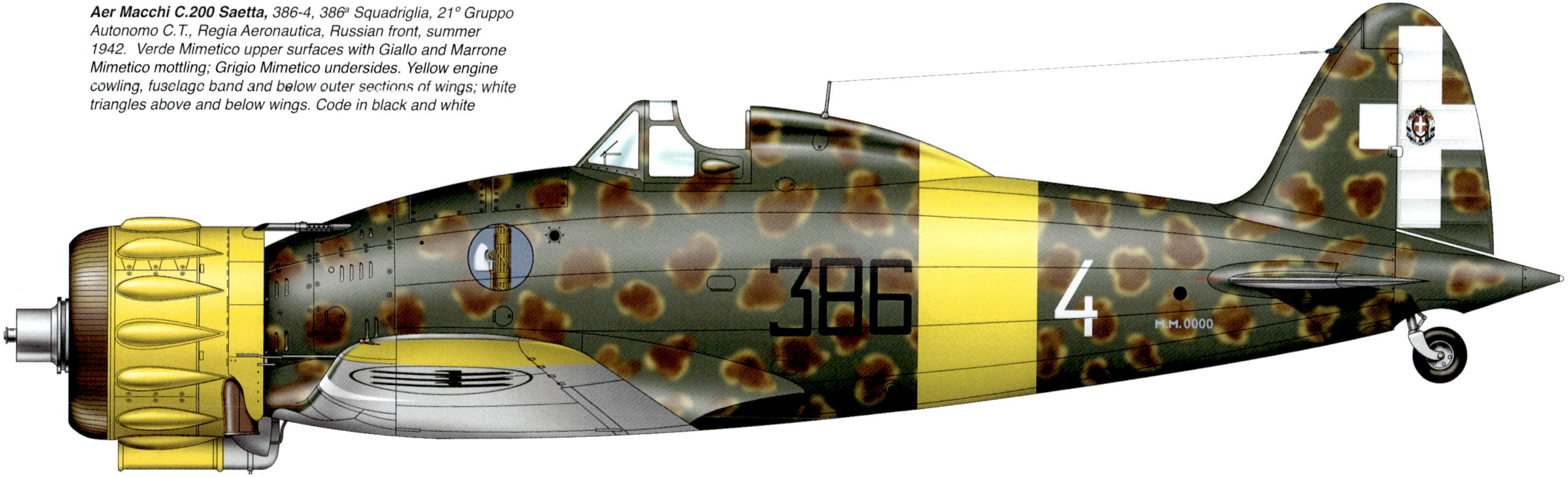

Aer Macchi C.200 Saetta, *356-1, 356ª Squadriglia, 21° Gruppo Autonomo C.T., Regia Aeronautica, Kosovo summer 1942. Verde Mimetico upper surfaces with mottling of Giallo Mimetico with Grigio Mimetico undersides. Yellow engine cowling, fuselage band and below outer sections of wings; white triangles above and below wings. Codes are all black and white. Unit badge below windscreen, both sides (other side the badge is flipped*

Aer Macchi C.200 Saetta 'Cineavia', *382-10, 382ª Squadriglia, 21° Gruppo Autonomo, Voroscilovgrad (Russia), July 1942. Verde Mimetico upper surfaces with Giallo Mimetico 3 mottling; Grigio Mimetico undersides. Yellow engine cowling, fuselage band and below outer sections of wings; white triangles above and below wings. Code in black and white; unit badge on forward fuselage. Black outline markings above wings; white markings on a black background below wings. Note lack of fuselage fasces insignia. This aircraft was equipped with cine cameras (believed to be on both sides) and the cowling is missing the bottom cooling gill on the other side (see photo p.32)*

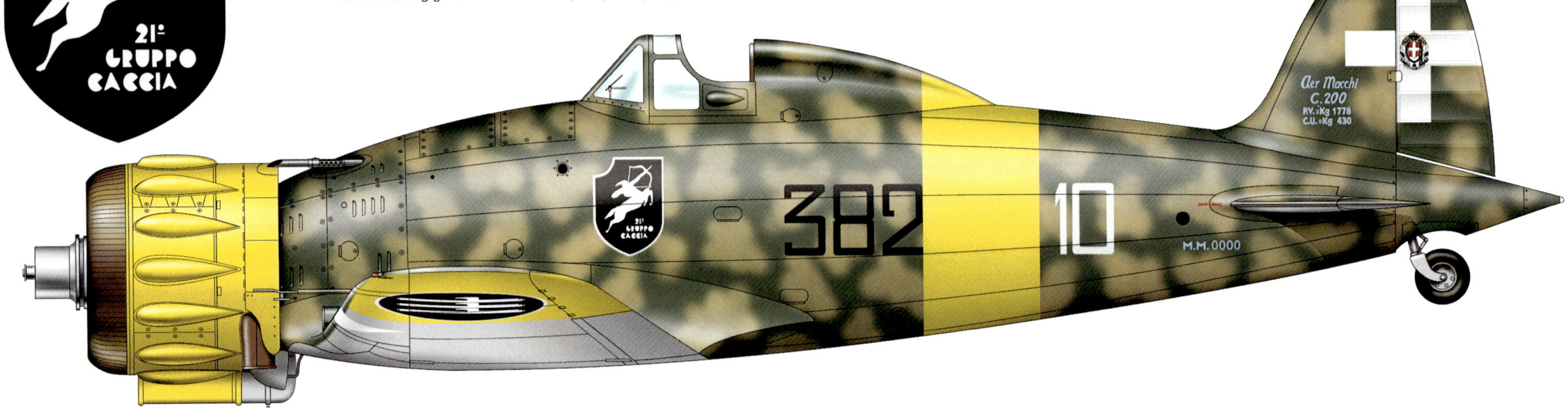

***Aer Macchi C.200 Saetta,** 382-13, 382ª Squadriglia, 21° Gruppo Autonomo, Voroscilovgrad (Russia), July 1942. Giallo Mimetico with Verde Mimetico mottling on upper surfaces with Grigio Mimetico undersides. Yellow engine cowling, fuselage band and below outer sections of wings; white triangles above and below wings. Code in black and white. Black outline markings above and below wings. Large areas of Verde Mimetico were applied over the fuselage to cover its previous identity markings*

***Aer Macchi C.200 Saetta,** 382-6, 382ª Squadriglia, 21° Gruppo Autonomo C.T., Voroshilovgrad, July 1942. Verde Oliva Scuro 2 upper surfaces with undersides in Grigio Azzuro Chiaro 1. Yellow engine cowling, rear fuselage band and underside of wingtips. Black national markings in four wing positions, white triangels on wing leading edges, above and below. Codes in black and white*

***Aer Macchi C.200 Saetta,** 369-11, flown by capitano Giorgio Iannicelli, Commander of 369ª Squadriglia, 22° Gruppo Autonomo C.T., Stalino (Russia), December 1941. Verde Mimetico upper surfaces with Giallo and Marrone Mimetico mottling; Grigio Mimetico undersides. Yellow cowling, fuselage band and below outer sections of wings; white triangles above and below wings. White disk on rear fuselage. Codes in black and red. Iannicelli was killed in action on 29 December 1941*

***Aer Macchi C.200 Saetta,** 369-11, flown by capitano Giovanni Cerulean, Commander of 369ª Squadriglia, 22° Gruppo Autonomo C.T., Stalino (Russia), February 1942. Verde Mimetico upper surfaces with Giallo and Marrone Mimetico mottling; Grigio Mimetico undersides. Yellow fuselage band and below outer sections of wings; white triangles above and below wings. Codes in black and white. Unit badge on forward fuselage (without the red background)*

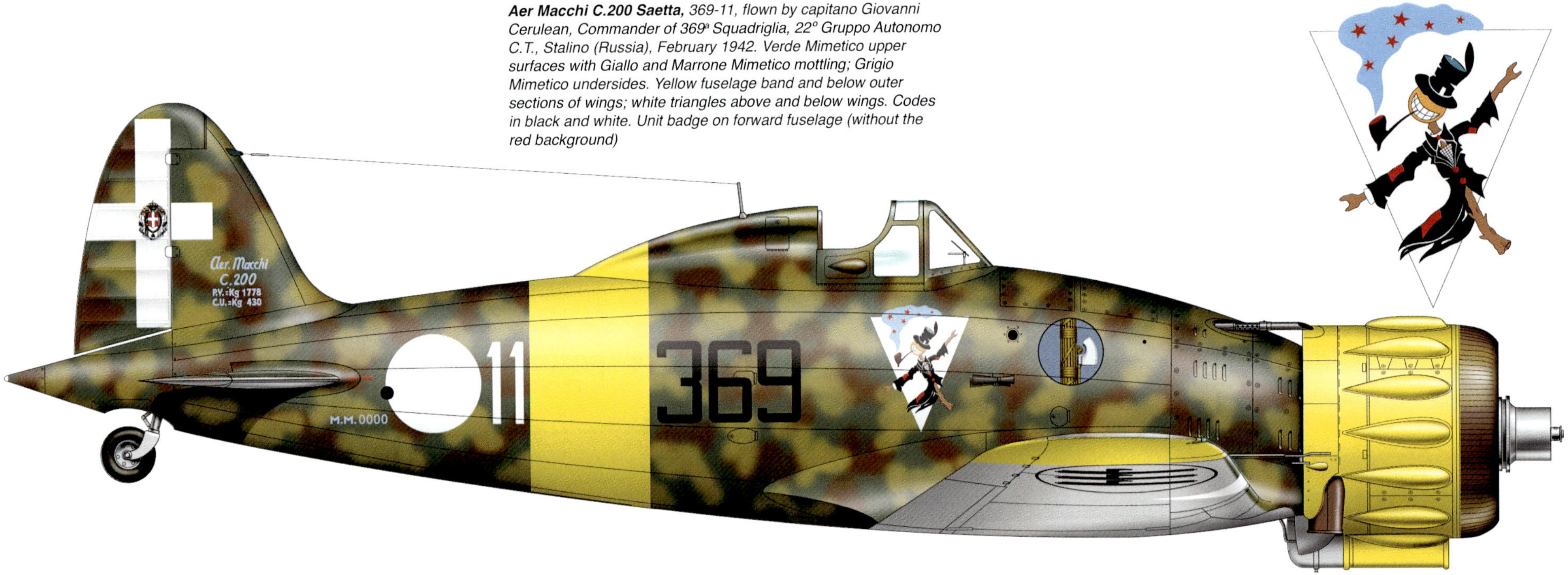

Aer Macchi C.200 Saetta, *386-5, 386ª Squadriglia, 21° Gruppo Autonomo C.T., Regia Aeronautica, Voroshilovgrad, summer 1942. Verde Mimetico upper surfaces with Giallo and Marrone Mimetico mottling; Grigio Mimetico undersides. Yellow engine cowling, rear fuselage band and underside of wingtips. White triangles on leading edges of wings, above and below. Codes in black and white. Small style tail cross in plain white*

Aer Macchi C.200 Saetta, *356-4, 356a Squadriglia, 21° Gruppo Autonomo C.T., Regia Aeronautica, Kosovo, summer 1942. Original verde Mimetico upper surfaces with mottling of Giallo Mimetico overpainted in Verde Oliva Scuro 2, with the previous finish showing through especially towards the rear fuselage and tail; Grigio Azzurro Chiaro 1 undersides. Yellow engine cowling, fuselage band and below outer sections of wings; white triangles above and below wings. Codes are all black and white. Unit badge below windscreen, both sides*

Aer Macchi C.200 Saetta, *356-13, 356ª Squadriglia, 21° Gruppo Autonomo C.T. Regia Aeronautica, summer 1942. Verde Mimetico upper surfaces with Giallo Mimetico mottling, Grigio Mimetico undersides. Yellow engine cowling, rear fuselage band and undersides of wingtips. Codes in black and white. White triangles on leading edges, below and above wings. Unit badge on forward fuselage, both sides*

Aer Macchi C.200 Saetta Serie XXIII, *M.M.8597A.S., 356-18, 356ª Squadriglia, 21° Gruppo AutonomoC.T Regia Aeronautica, Kantemirowska (Russia), November 1942. Verde Oliva 2 on all upper surfaces with Grigio Azzurro Chiaro undersides. Yellow engine cowling, fuselage band and below outer sections of wings; white triangles above and below wings. Codes in black and white. Note '6' in red on mainwheel undercarriage doors*

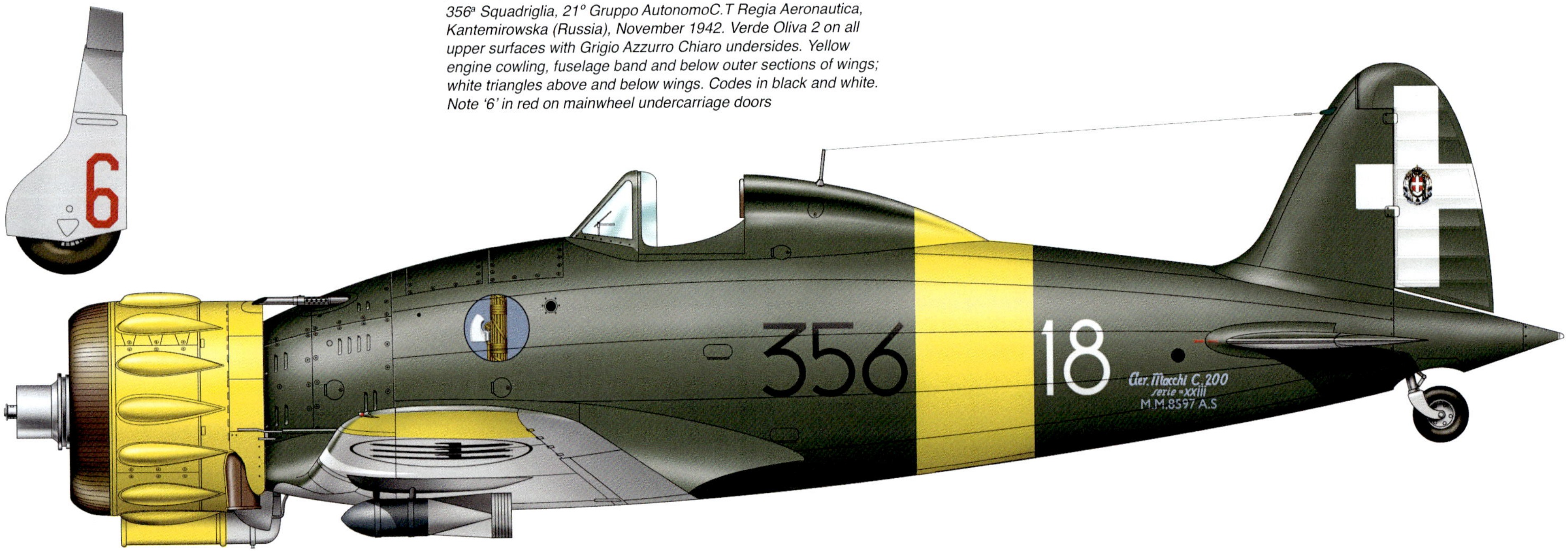

***Aer Macchi C.200 Saetta,** 369-10, 369ª Squadriglia, 22° Gruppo Autonomo C.T. Regia Aeronautica, Stalino 1943, reportedly captured by Soviet forces. Verde Mimetico upper surfaces with Giallo and Marrone Mimetico mottling; Grigio Mimetico undersides. Yellow fuselage band and below outer sections of wings; white triangles above and below wings. Codes in black and white. Unit badge below windscreen*

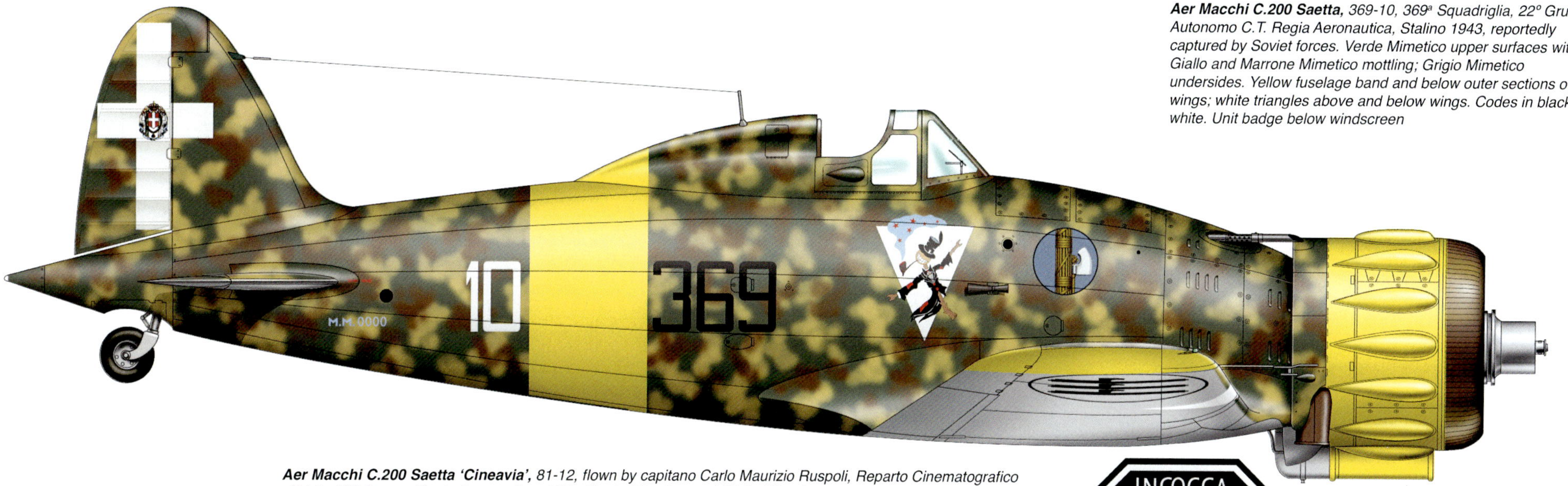

***Aer Macchi C.200 Saetta 'Cineavia',** 81-12, flown by capitano Carlo Maurizio Ruspoli, Reparto Cinematografico di Volo, 22° Gruppo Regia Aeronautica, 1941. Verde Mimetico and Giallo Mimetico upper surfaces with Grigio Mimetico undersides. White fuselage band with unit marking superimposed lboth sides), large white cross on vertical tail surfaces. Yellow underside outer sections of wings. White national markings above wings with black fasces, black below wings with white fasces. Codes in black and red. Note cine camera lens on wing leading edges (both sides) and tropical filter below the engine cowling. Three such aircraft were sent just a few days after the arrival of the C.200s on the Russian Front to film propaganda footage of their initial missions*

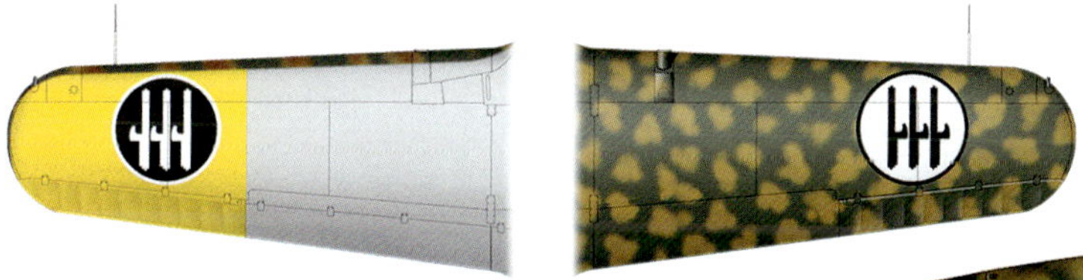

Aer Macchi C.202 Folgore, *356-1, 356ª Squadriglia, 21° Gruppo Autonomo, Kantemirowka (Russia), December 1942. Typical Breda factory finish on upper surfaces consisting of Nocciola Chiaro 4 with sparse mottles in Verde Oliva Scuro 2; Grigio Azzurro Chiaro 1 undersides. Yellow nose, fuselage band and undersides of wingtips; white triangles above and below wings. Code in black/white. From extensive study of photographs of C.202s operating on the Russian Front, it has been established that the unit badge was carried on this side of fin only*

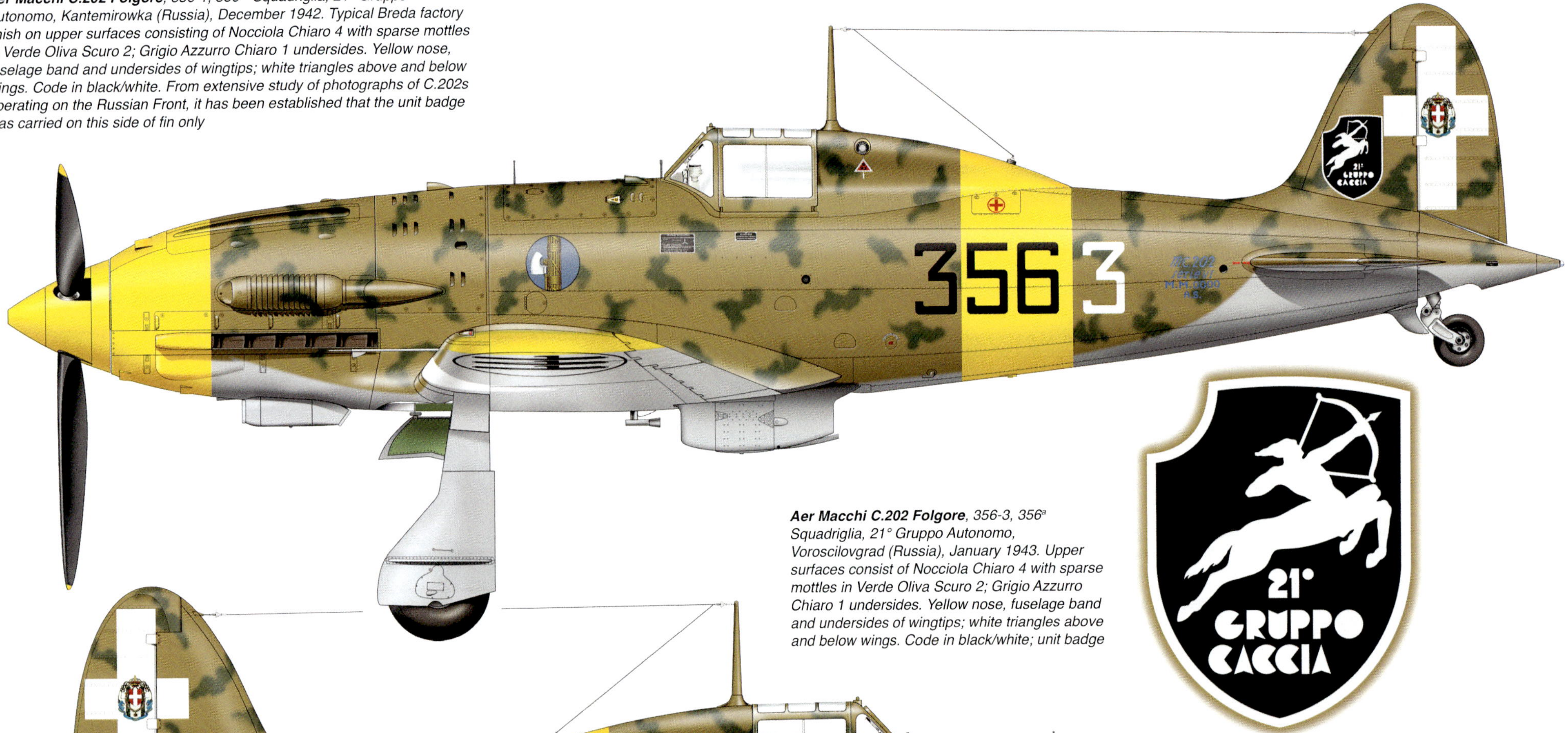

Aer Macchi C.202 Folgore, *356-3, 356ª Squadriglia, 21° Gruppo Autonomo, Voroscilovgrad (Russia), January 1943. Upper surfaces consist of Nocciola Chiaro 4 with sparse mottles in Verde Oliva Scuro 2; Grigio Azzurro Chiaro 1 undersides. Yellow nose, fuselage band and undersides of wingtips; white triangles above and below wings. Code in black/white; unit badge*

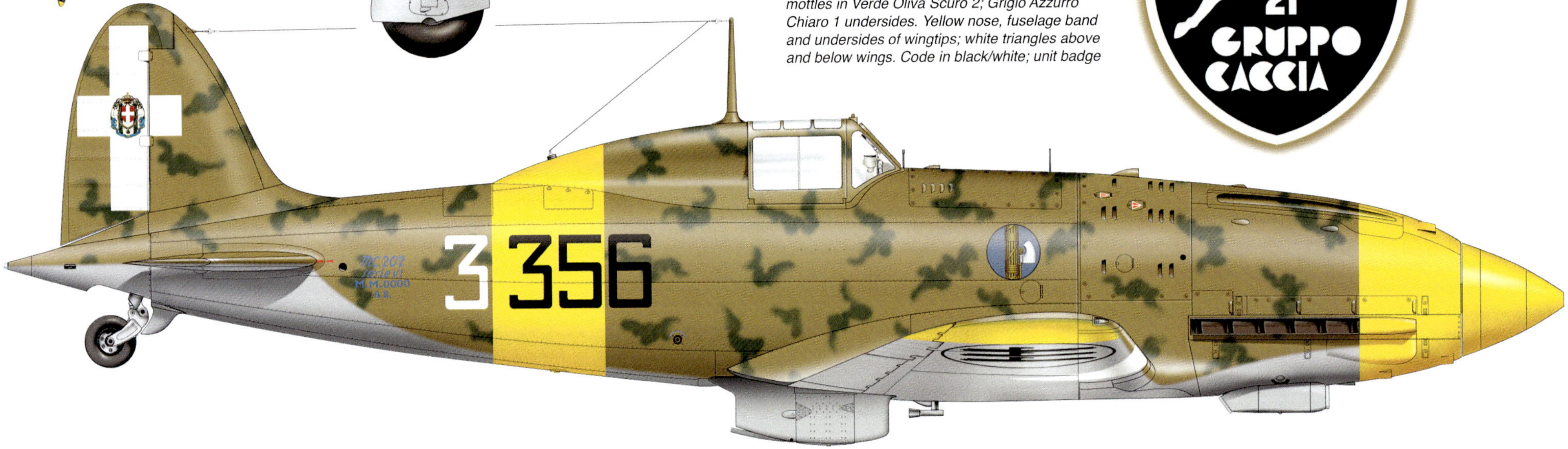

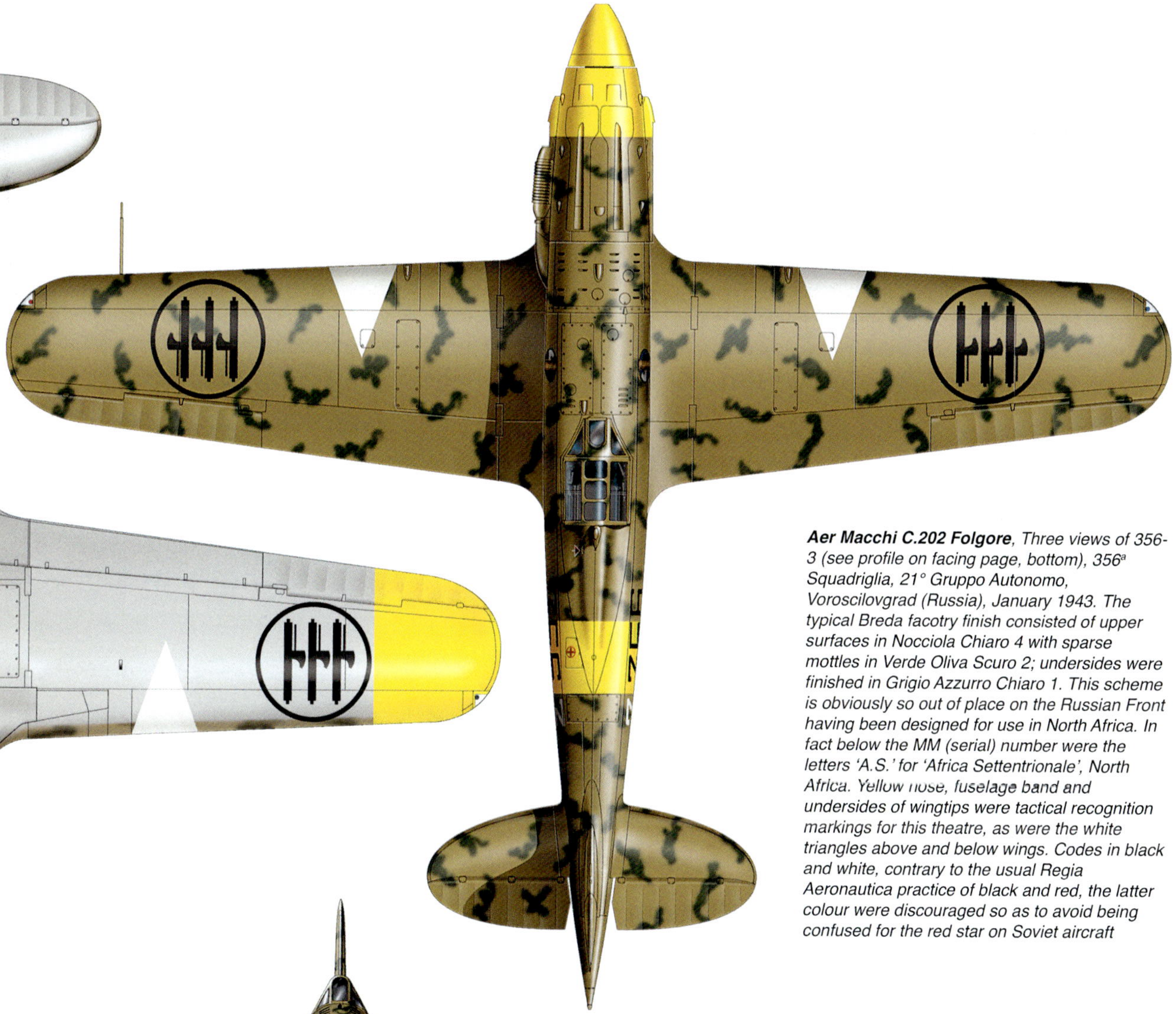

***Aer Macchi C.202 Folgore**, Three views of 356-3 (see profile on facing page, bottom), 356ª Squadriglia, 21° Gruppo Autonomo, Voroscilovgrad (Russia), January 1943. The typical Breda facotry finish consisted of upper surfaces in Nocciola Chiaro 4 with sparse mottles in Verde Oliva Scuro 2; undersides were finished in Grigio Azzurro Chiaro 1. This scheme is obviously so out of place on the Russian Front having been designed for use in North Africa. In fact below the MM (serial) number were the letters 'A.S.' for 'Africa Settentrionale', North Africa. Yellow nose, fuselage band and undersides of wingtips were tactical recognition markings for this theatre, as were the white triangles above and below wings. Codes in black and white, contrary to the usual Regia Aeronautica practice of black and red, the latter colour were discouraged so as to avoid being confused for the red star on Soviet aircraft*

Aer Macchi C.202 Folgore, *361-3 361ª Squadriglia, 21° Gruppo Autonomo, Kantemirowka (Russia), Autumn 1942. Typical Breda factory finish on upper surfaces consisting of Nocciola Chiaro 4 with sparse mottles in Verde Oliva Scuro 2; Grigio Azzurro Chiaro 1 undersides. Yellow nose, fuselage band and undersides of wingtips; white triangles above and below wings. Code in black/white. Note Aeronuatica Macchi series and weight legend on fin in Savoy Blue, as on all serial number legends ahead of tailplane on all Macchi fighters*

Aer Macchi C.202 Folgore, *356-1, 356ª Squadriglia, 21° Gruppo Autonomo, Kantemirowka (Russia), November 1942. Typical Breda factory finish on upper surfaces consisting of Nocciola Chiaro 4 with sparse mottles in Verde Oliva Scuro 2; Grigio Azzurro Chiaro 1 undersides. Yellow nose, fuselage band and undersides of wingtips; white triangles above and below wings. Code in black/white; unit badge on other side of fin only*

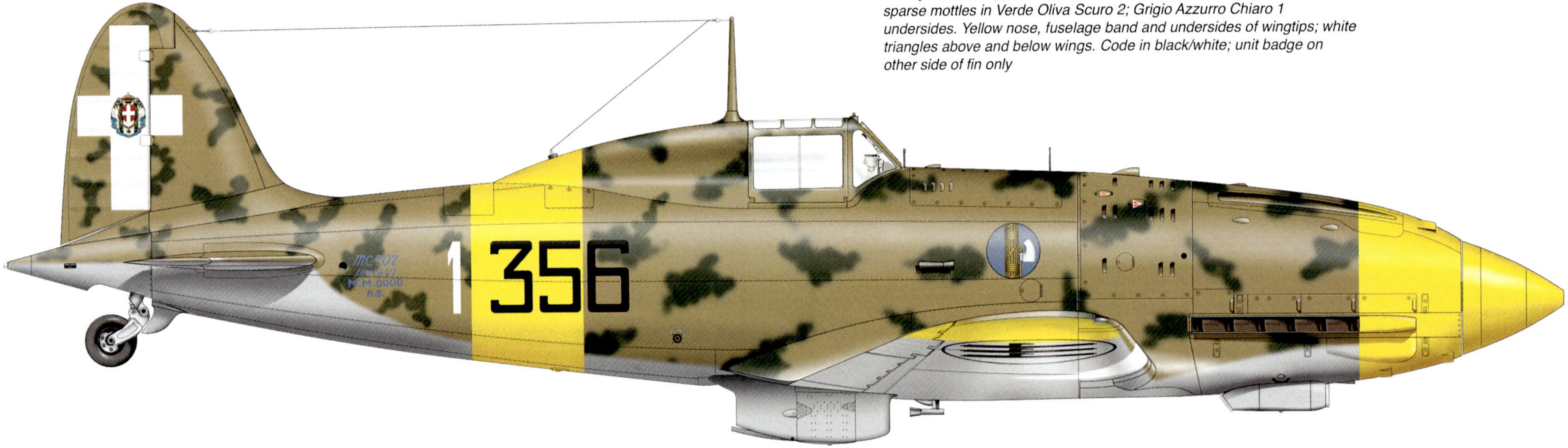

Aer Macchi C.202 Folgore, *382-3, 382ª Squadriglia, 21° Gruppo Autonomo, Kantemirowka (Russia), November 1942. Typical Breda factory finish on upper surfaces consisting of Nocciola Chiaro 4 with sparse mottles in Verde Oliva Scuro 2; Grigio Azzurro Chiaro 1 undersides. Yellow nose, fuselage band and undersides of wingtips; white triangles above and below wings. Code in black/white; unit badge on other side of fin only*

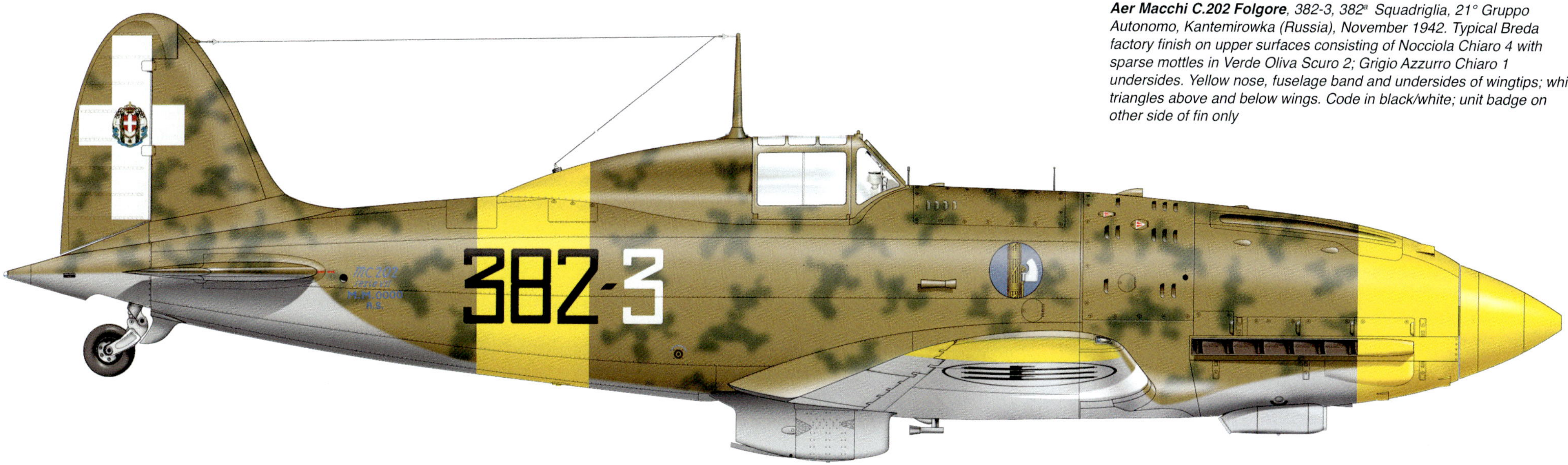

Aer Macchi C.202 Folgore Serie VI, *M.M..8122/386-1, 386ª Squadriglia, 21° Gruppo Autonomo, Kantemirowka (Russia), Autumn 1942. Typical Breda factory finish on upper surfaces consisting of Nocciola Chiaro 4 with sparse mottles in Verde Oliva Scuro 2; Grigio Azzurro Chiaro 1 undersides. Yellow nose, fuselage band and undersides of wingtips; white triangles above and below wings. Code in black/white; unit badge on fin, port side only*

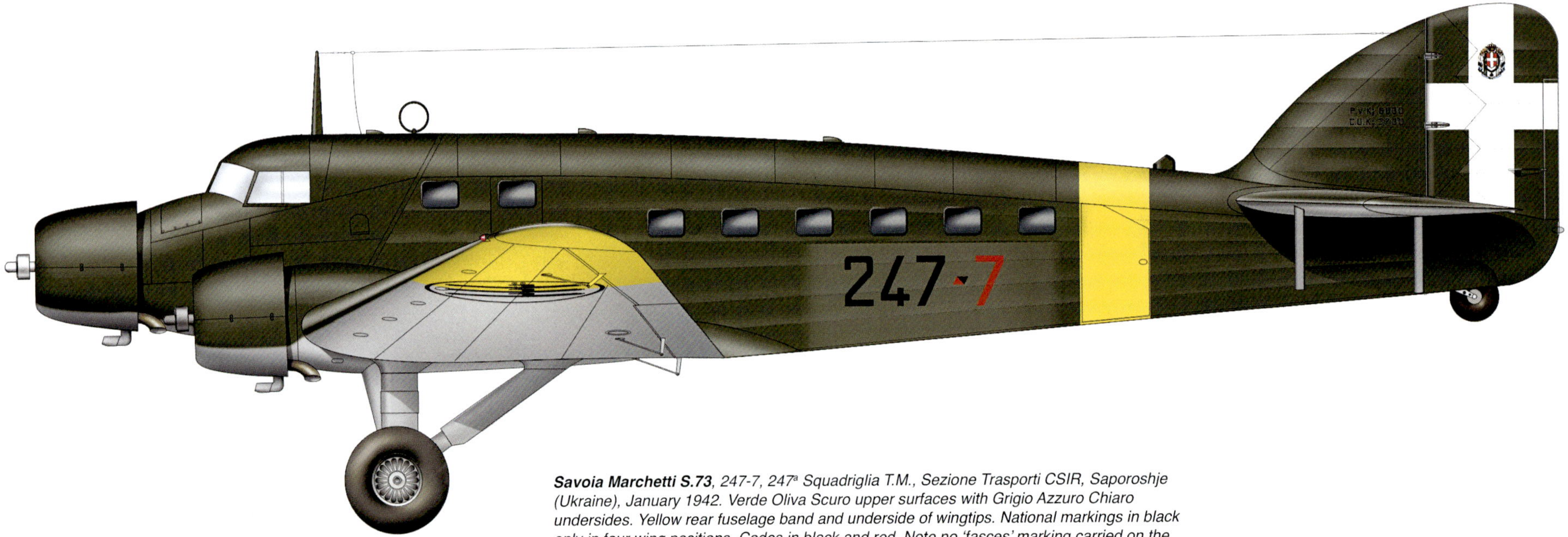

Savoia Marchetti S.73, *247-7, 247ª Squadriglia T.M., Sezione Trasporti CSIR, Saporoshje (Ukraine), January 1942. Verde Oliva Scuro upper surfaces with Grigio Azzuro Chiaro undersides. Yellow rear fuselage band and underside of wingtips. National markings in black only in four wing positions. Codes in black and red. Note no 'fasces' marking carried on the nose; also, previous civil identity codes overpainted on fuselage sides*

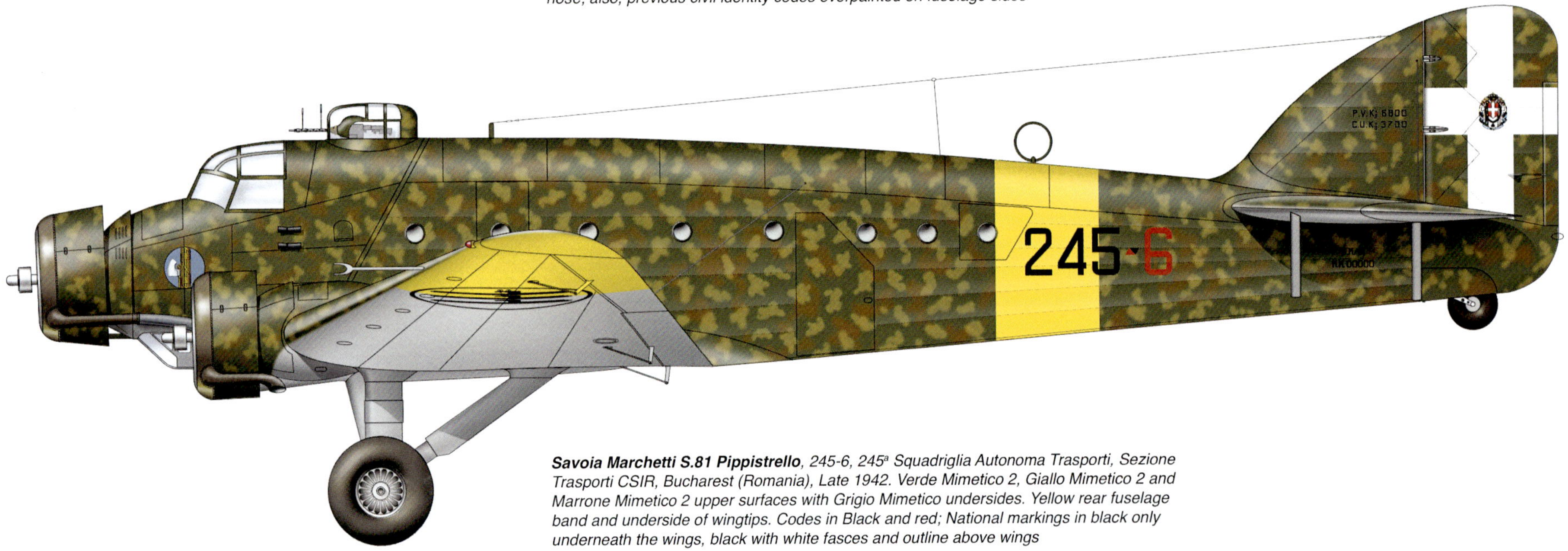

Savoia Marchetti S.81 Pippistrello, *245-6, 245ª Squadriglia Autonoma Trasporti, Sezione Trasporti CSIR, Bucharest (Romania), Late 1942. Verde Mimetico 2, Giallo Mimetico 2 and Marrone Mimetico 2 upper surfaces with Grigio Mimetico undersides. Yellow rear fuselage band and underside of wingtips. Codes in Black and red; National markings in black only underneath the wings, black with white fasces and outline above wings*

***Savoia Marchetti S.81 Pippistrello**, 246-2, 246ª Squadriglia T.M., Sezione Trasporti CSIR, Saporoshje (Ukraine), Late 1942. Verde Oliva Scuro uppersurfaces with Grigio Azzurro Chiaro undersides. Yellow rear fuselage band and underside of wingtips. Codes in Black and red; note unusual position of the individual numner '2' aft of the unit number on the starboard side. National markings in black only in four wing positions. Unit badge on port side only.*

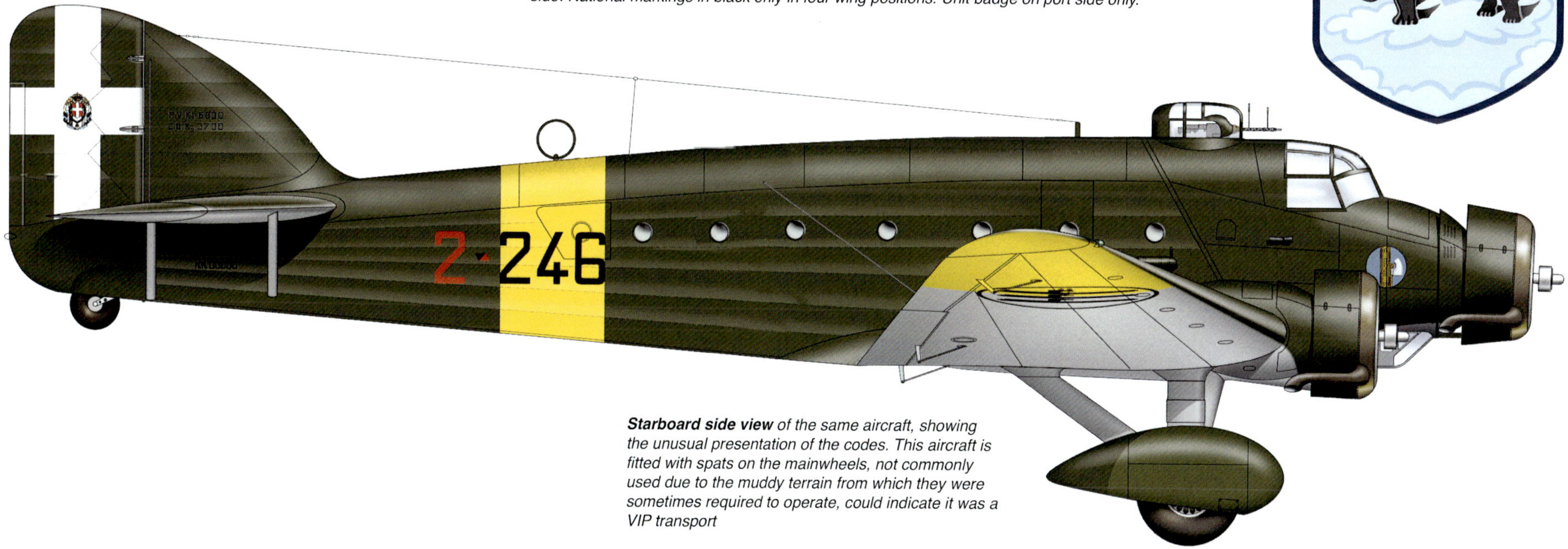

***Starboard side view** of the same aircraft, showing the unusual presentation of the codes. This aircraft is fitted with spats on the mainwheels, not commonly used due to the muddy terrain from which they were sometimes required to operate, could indicate it was a VIP transport*

Savoia Marchetti S.81 Pippistrello, *M.M.20759. 246-7, 246ª Squadriglia T.M., Sezione Trasporti CSIR, Saporoshje (Ukraine), Late 1942. Verde Mimetico 2, Giallo Mimetico 2 and Marrone Mimetico 2 upper surfaces with Grigio Mimetico undersides. Yellow rear fuselage band and underside of wingtips. Codes in Black and red. National markings in black only underneath the wings, black with white fasces and outline above wings. Unit badge on port side only*

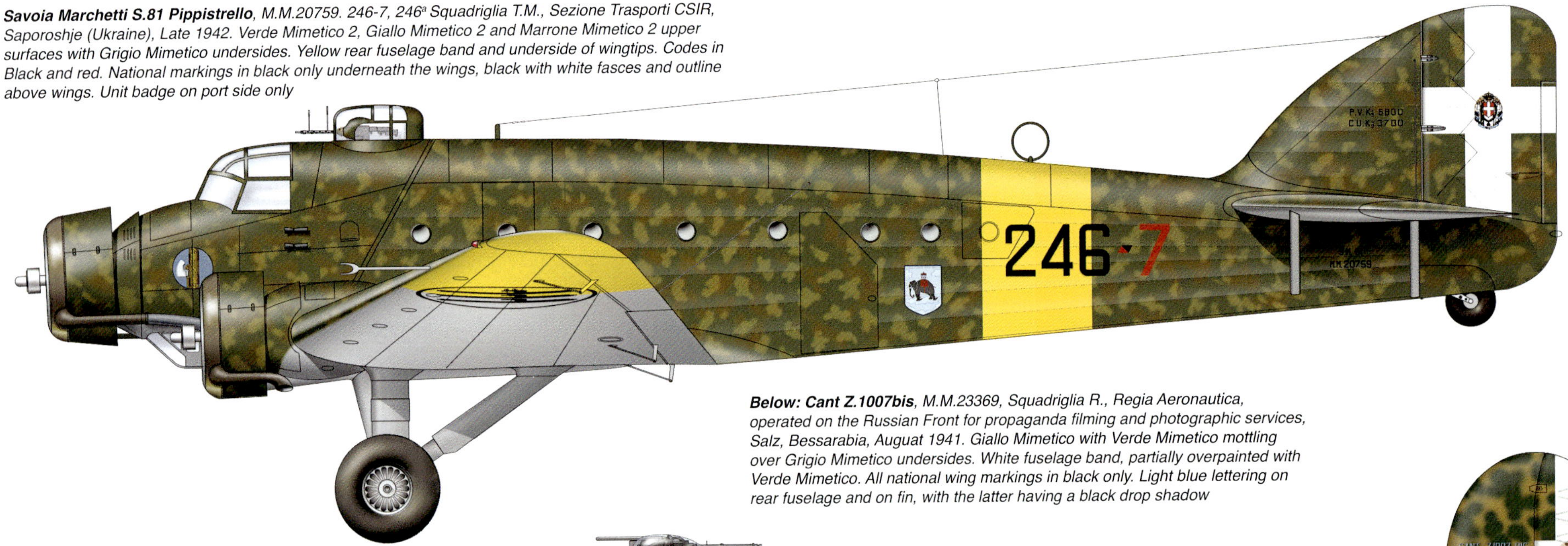

Below: Cant Z.1007bis, *M.M.23369, Squadriglia R., Regia Aeronautica, operated on the Russian Front for propaganda filming and photographic services, Salz, Bessarabia, Auguat 1941. Giallo Mimetico with Verde Mimetico mottling over Grigio Mimetico undersides. White fuselage band, partially overpainted with Verde Mimetico. All national wing markings in black only. Light blue lettering on rear fuselage and on fin, with the latter having a black drop shadow*

FIAT BR.20M Cicogna, *116-2 (MM unknown), 116ª Squadrigilia, 71° Gruppo Osservazione Aerea, Millerovo (Russia), autumn 1942. Verde Oliva Scuro upper surfaces with Grigio Azzurro Chiaro undersides. Yellow fuselage band; codes in black and red. National markings in black only, above and below wings*

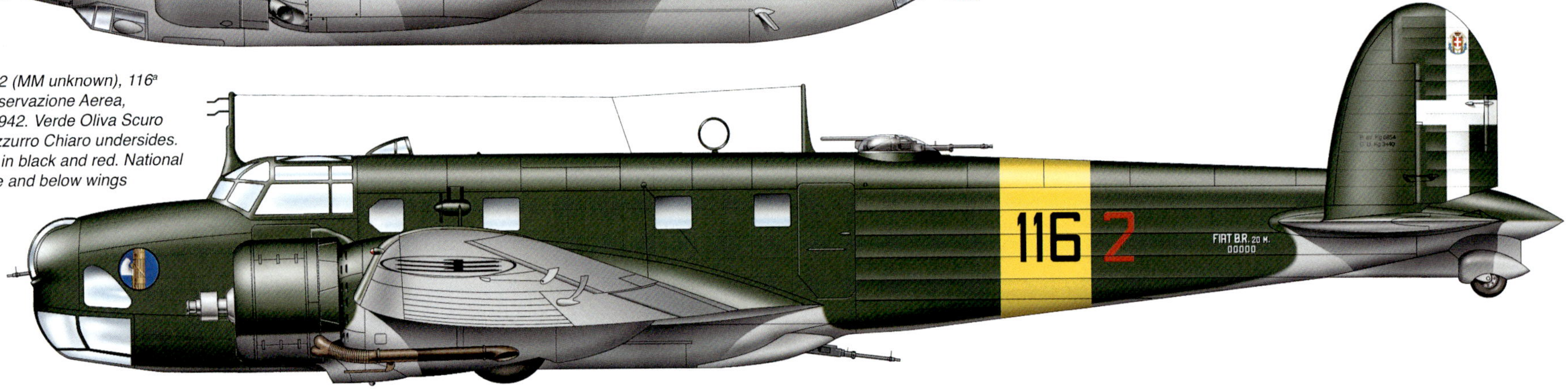

Caproni Ca.311, *128-2, 128ª Squadriglia, 61° Gruppo Osservazione Aerea, Saproroshje, November 1941. Verde Mimetico and Giallo Mimetico upper surfaces with Grgio Mimctico undersides. Yellow fuselage band and undersides of wingtips. Codes in black and red. National markings above and below wings in black only*

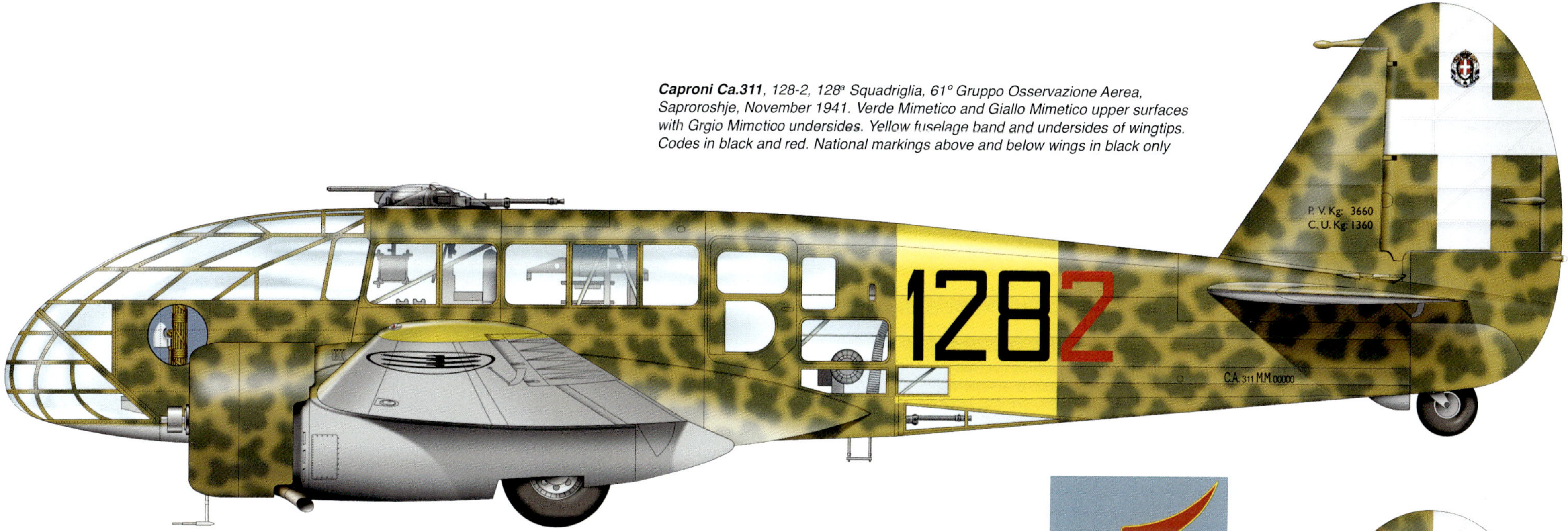

Caproni Ca.311M, *34-7, 34ª Squadriglia, 61° Gruppo Osservazione Aerea, Krivol Rog (Russia), 1942. Giallo Mimetico, Verde Mimetico and Marrone Mimetico upper surfaces with Grigio Mimetico undersides. Yellow fuselage band, engine cowlings and underside of wingtips. Codes in black and red. Wing national markings in black only. Unit's badge consisting of a red winged horse over a yellow background on fin, both sides*

***Caproni Ca.311M**, 38-4, 38ª Squadriglia, 71° Gruppo, Stalin airport (East Ukraine), summer 1942. Verde Oliva Scuro upper surfaces with Grigio Azzurro Chiaro undersdies. Yellow fuselage band and undersides of wingtips. Codes in black and red. National wing markings in black only*

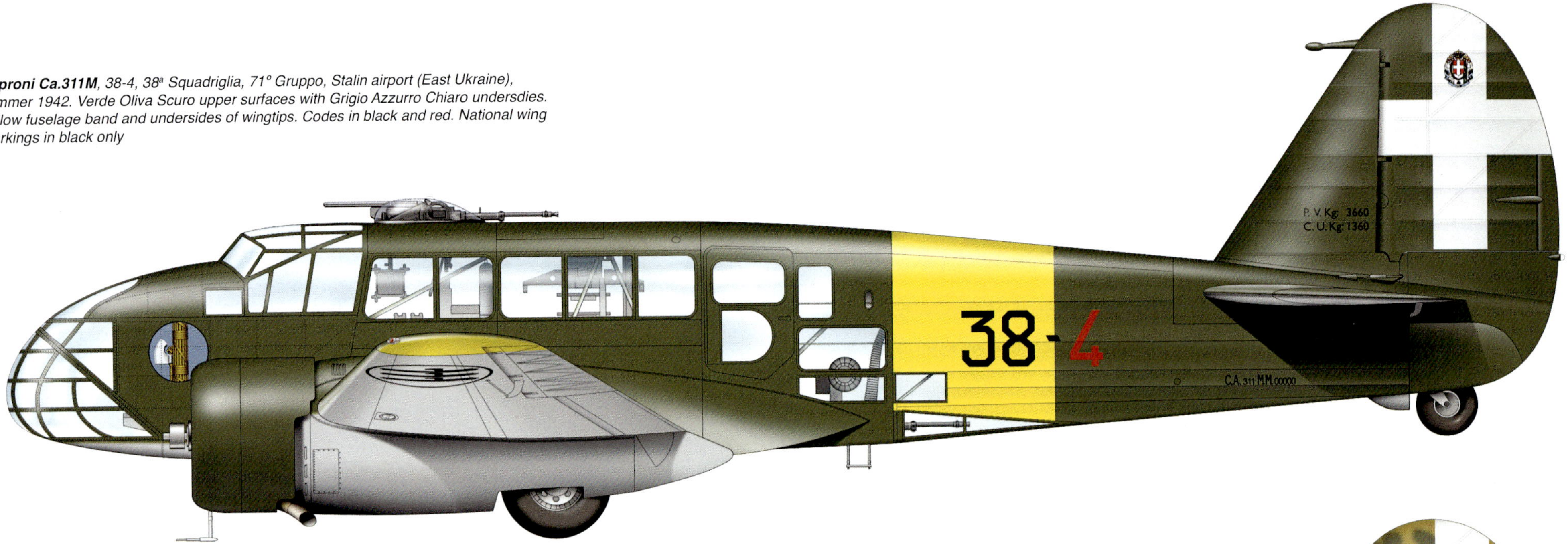

***Caproni Ca.311M**, 83-4, 116-2, 116ª Squadriglia, 71° Gruppo, Stalino (Eastern Ukraine), autumn 1941. Giallo Mimetico with Verde Mimetico upper surfaces Grigio Mimetico undersides. Yellow fuselage band and undersides of wingtips. Codes in black and red. National wing markings in black only*

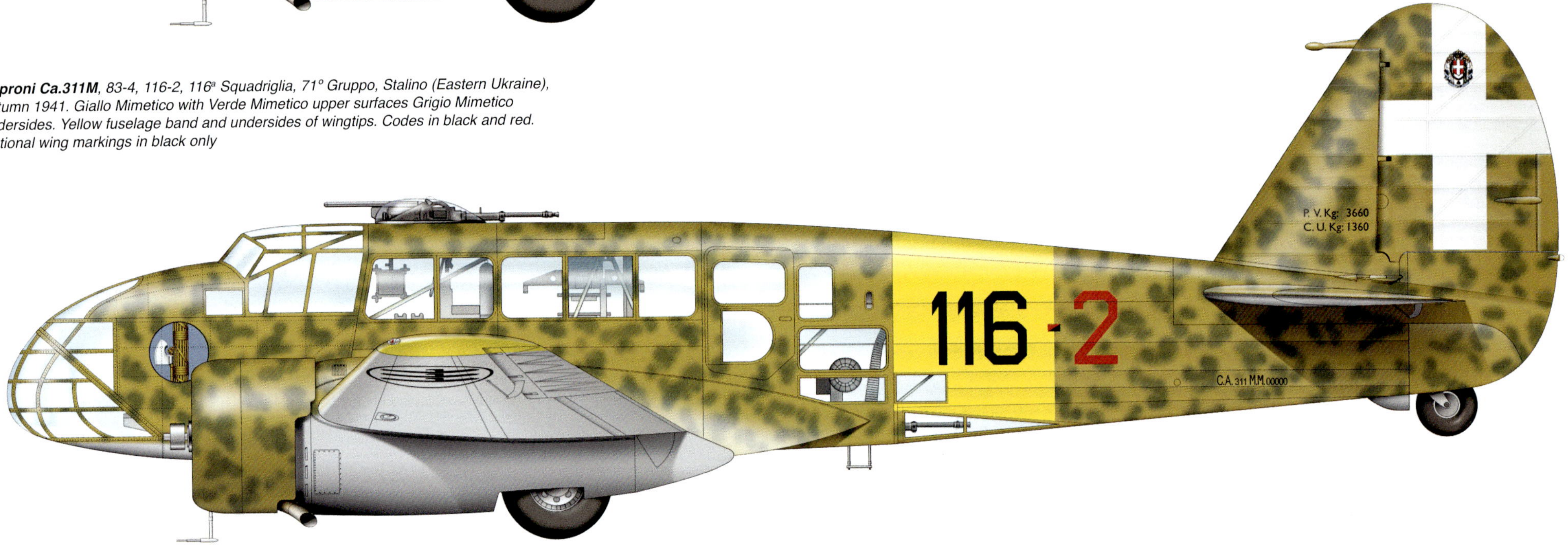

Caproni Ca.311M, *38-6, 38ª Squadriglia, 71° Gruppo, Stalin airport (East Ukraine), summer 1942. Verde Oliva Scuro upper surfaces with Grigio Azzurro Chiaro undersdies. Yellow fuselage band and undersides of wingtips. Codes in black and red. National wing markings in black only*

Caproni Ca.312bis, *M.M.12343, Servizi Ambulanza of the Regia Aeronautica, used for evacuation of injured personnel. Bianco Avorio (Ivory White) overall with Red Cross markings on fuselage sides. Green/white/red rudder and bands around wings. One of 24 unarmed examples of the type originally destined for Belgium, a small number of which were converted as flying ambulances*

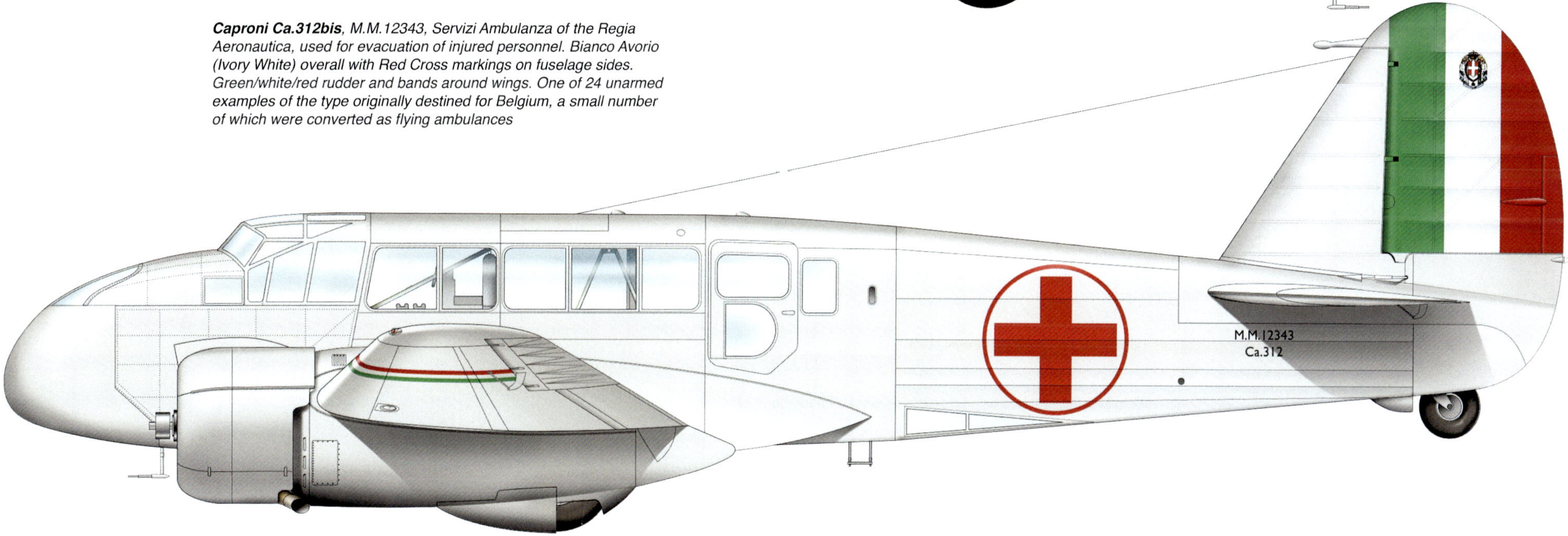

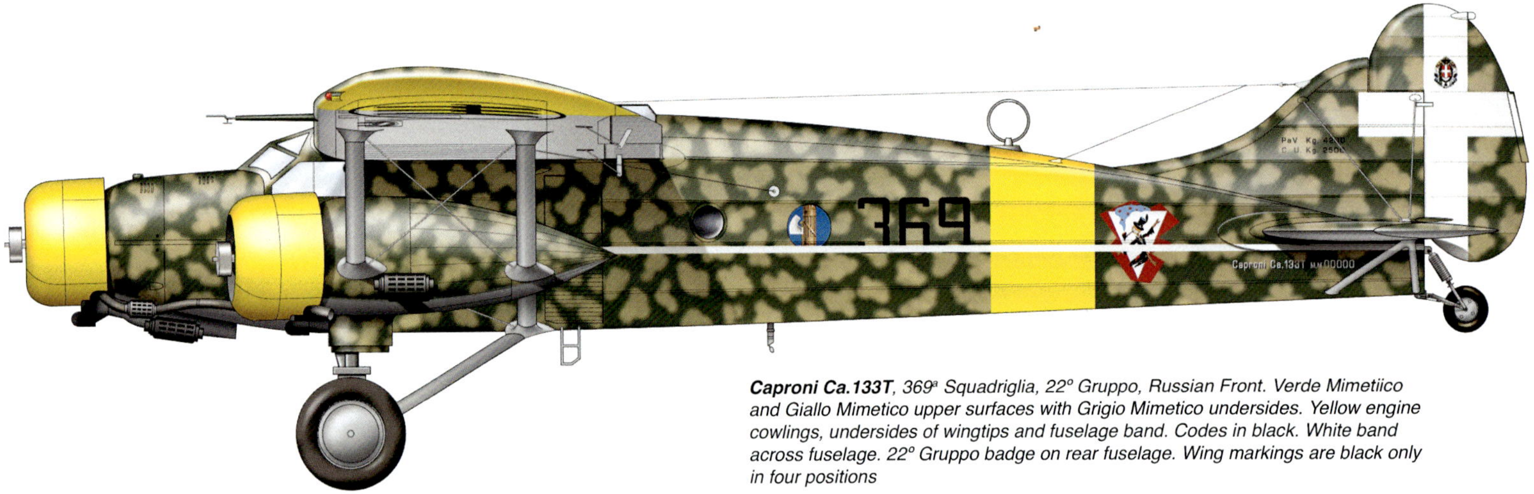

Caproni Ca.133T*, 369ª Squadriglia, 22º Gruppo, Russian Front. Verde Mimetiico and Giallo Mimetico upper surfaces with Grigio Mimetico undersides. Yellow engine cowlings, undersides of wingtips and fuselage band. Codes in black. White band across fuselage. 22º Gruppo badge on rear fuselage. Wing markings are black only in four positions*

ORDER OF BATTLE: Corpo di Spedizione Italiano in Russia

22º Gruppo Caccia Terrestre			
359ª, 362ª, 369ª, 371ª Squadriglia	08/1941	Aermacchi C.200	Tudora/Krivoi Rog
	10/1941	Aermacchi C.200	Saporischschja
21º Gruppo Caccia Terrestre			
356ª, 361ª, 386ª Squadriglie	04/1942	Aermacchi C.200	Stalino
356ª, 361ª, 382ª, 386ª Squadriglie	07/1942	Aermacchi C.200	Voroscilovgrad/Makejevka
	01/1943	Aermacchi C.200	Stalino/Saporischschja
	02/1943	Aermacchi C.200	Odessa
356ª, 361ª, 382ª, 386ª Squadriglie	1942/43	AerMacchi C.202	Kantemirowka/Voroscilovgrad
71º Gruppo Osservazione Aerea			
38ª, 116ª Squadriglie	05/1942	Caproni Ca.311; Ca.312	Stalino
	08/1942	Caproni Ca.311; Ca.312. FIAT BR.20M	Voroscilovgrad
	02/1943	Caproni Ca.311; Ca.312;Ca.164 FIAT BR.20M	Stalino
	1943	Caproni Ca.311; Ca.312. FIAT BR.20M	Saporischschja/Odessa
61º Gruppo Osservazione Aerea			
34ª, 119ª, 128ª Squadriglie	08/1941	Caproni Ca.311	Tudora/Krivoi Rog
	11/1941	Caproni Ca.311	Stalino
Sezione Trasporti CSIR			
247ª Squadriglia	01/1942	Savoia Marchetti S.73	Saporischschja
245ª, 246ª Squadriglia	12/1942	Savoia Marchetti S.81	Saporischschja